July

Making Books with Pockets

The series of monthly activity books you've been waiting for!

Enliven every month of the year with fun, exciting learning projects that students can proudly present in a unique book format.

Each month has lessons for art, writing, reading, math, science, social studies, and poetry.

Contents

Michelle Barnett, Caitlin Rabanera, and **Ann Switzer** have taught first, second, and third grade. Their teaching experiences have involved working with limited-English-speaking students from many parts of the world, supervising student teachers, and conducting inservice sessions for colleagues. They are currently teaching in Southern California.

Congratulations on your purchase of some of the finest teaching materials in the world.

For information about other Evan-Moor products, call 1-800-777-4362 or FAX 1-800-777-4332

Visit our website http://www.evan-moor.com. Check the Product Updates link for supplements, additions, and corrections for this book.

Authors:	Michelle Barnett
	Caitlin Rabanera
	Ann Switzer
Editors:	Marilyn Evans
	Jill Norris
Copy Editor:	Cathy Harber
Illustrator:	Jo Larsen
Designer:	Cheryl Puckett
Desktop:	Shannon Frederickson

Entire contents ©1999 by EVAN-MOOR CORP.
18 Lower Ragsdale Drive, Monterey, CA 93940-5746.
Permission is hereby granted to the individual purchaser to reproduce student materials in this book for noncommercial individual or classroom use only. Permission is not granted for schoolwide, or systemwide, reproduction of materials.
Printed in U.S.A.

Evan-Moor
EDUCATIONAL PUBLISHERS
EMC 590

July's Special Days

Here are ideas for celebrating some of the other special days in July.

July 1 _____ **Canada Day (Dominion Day)**
On this day, Canadians celebrate their independence with parades and picnics. Locate Canada on a map of North America. Display a picture of the Canadian flag. Have any students been to Canada? Share information about our neighbor to the north.

July 6 _____ **Beatrix Potter's Birthday**
Read *The Tale of Peter Rabbit* or one of Ms. Potter's other stories.

July 20 _____ **Moon Day**
U.S. astronaut Neil A. Armstrong became the first person to walk on the moon in 1969. Read a book about the first walk. Have students write a story about what they would do if they were the first to walk on the moon. Put it in the last pocket of the space book.

July 23 _____**Ice-Cream Cone Invented, 1904**
This happy event occurred at the World's Fair in St. Louis, Missouri. The ice-cream vendor ran out of dishes. The waffle vendor next to him began to roll his waffles in the shape of a cone to contain the cold confection. And, as they say, the rest is history! What else?...celebrate with ice-cream cones!

July 31 _____ **Tennis Comes to America**
Tennis was invented in England and brought to the United States in 1874 by Mary Ewing Outerbridge. Customs officials seized the rackets, balls, and net—they thought they were weapons! Brainstorm and list games that use nets, rackets, or balls.

National Baked Bean Month
Invite families to share their favorite recipes for baked beans. Compile the recipes in a cookbook to take home. Cook up a few varieties and have a baked bean tasting.

Anti-Boredom Month
Talk about what causes students to feel bored. Brainstorm some inventive solutions to boredom.

July

Sunday	Monday	Tuesday	Wednesday	Thursday	Friday	Saturday

How to Make Pocket Books

Each pocket book has a cover and three or more pockets. Choose construction paper colors that are appropriate to the theme of the book. Using several colors in a book creates an effective presentation.

other pockets

pocket 1

Materials

- 12" x 18" (30.5 x 45.5 cm) piece of construction paper for each pocket
- cover as described for each book
- hole punch
- stapler
- string, ribbon, twine, raffia, etc., for ties

Steps to Follow

1. Fold the construction paper to create a pocket. After folding, the paper should measure 12" (30.5 cm) square.

2. Staple the right side of each pocket closed.

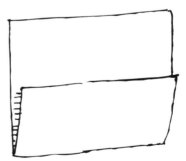

3. Punch two or three holes in the left side of each pocket and the cover.

4. Fasten the book together using your choice of material as ties.

5. Glue the poem or information strips onto each pocket as shown on the overview pages of each book.

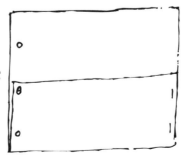

America, the Beautiful

What better month than July to talk about the symbols of our nation? Students will learn about the "Stars and Stripes," the Statue of Liberty, and Independence Day celebrations. They will complete colorful art projects, make minibooks, and find out about how their families came to America.

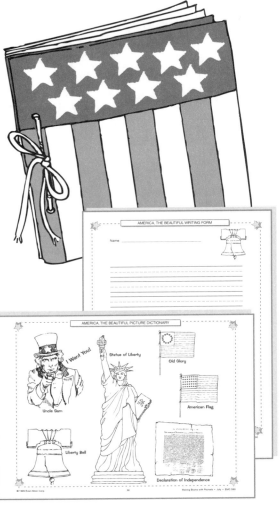

This poem can also be used for pocket chart activities throughout the month:
- Chant the poem
- Listen for rhyming words
- Learn new vocabulary
- Identify sight words
- Put words or lines in the correct order

Use the picture dictionary to introduce new vocabulary and as a spelling reference. Students can add new pictures, labels, and descriptive adjectives to the page as their vocabulary increases.

Use this form for story writing or as a place to record additional vocabulary words.

BIBLIOGRAPHY

Beat the Drum, Independence Day Has Come: Poems for the Fourth of July edited by Lee Bennett Hopkins; Boyds Mills, 1993.
Celebrating Independence Day by Shelly Nielsen; Abdo & Daughters, 1992.
Fireworks, Flags, and Picnics by James Cross Giblin; Houghton Mifflin, 1983.
A Flag for Our Country by Eve Spencer; Raintree Steck-Vaughn, 1993.
The Flag We Love by Pam Muñoz Ryan; Charlesbridge, 1996.
Hurray for the Fourth of July by Wendy Watson; Clarion Books, 1992.
The Statue of Liberty by Patricia Ryon Quiri; Children's Press, 1998.
The Story of the Statue of Liberty by Betsy & Giulio Maestro, Mulberry Books, 1989.

POCKET 1

Glittering Fireworks   **page 9**
Brightly colored fireworks made from glitter
on black paper provide the motivation for
writing cinquain verse.

Fireworks Cinquain   **pages 10–12**
Provide models of cinquain verse and then
guide students to create their own five-line
verses.

Torn-Paper Star   **pages 13 and 14**
These decorative stars can be hung around
the classroom before going into the pocket.

Fireworks crackle and light up the sky
On Independence Day—the 4th of July.

Our country has changed. Our flag has, too.
The stars number 50 on the field of blue.

POCKET 2

**The American Flag—
Then and Now**   **pages 15 and 16**
This color, cut, and paste project shows how
the United States flag has changed
since 1776.

**Things Weren't
Always Like This**   **pages 17–20**
Reproduce this minibook for students to put
together and then read about some of the
changes that have occurred in the last
200-plus years.

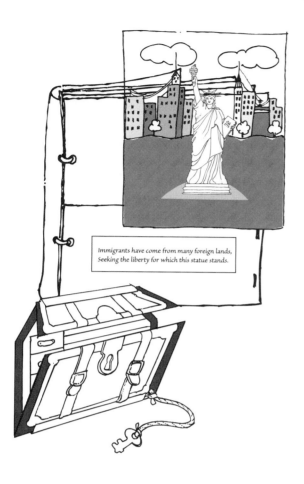

Immigrants have come from many foreign lands,
Seeking the liberty for which this statue stands.

The Statue of Liberty   **pages 21 and 22**
This cut-paper art project shows the Statue of Liberty with a city skyline in the background.

Coming to America   **pages 23–26**
Students make a book in the shape of a trunk and write about how their families came to America.

America, the Beautiful Songbook   **pages 27–33**
This truly special six-page book presents visuals to accompany the words to the song. Students will be anxious to sing along!

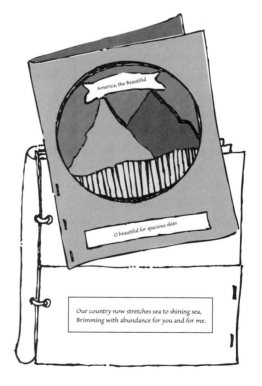

America, the Beautiful

O beautiful for spacious skies

Our country now stretches sea to shining sea,
Brimming with abundance for you and for me.

Materials

- construction paper

  background—white, 12" (30.5 cm) square
  field—blue, 4" x 12" (10 x 30.5 cm)
  stripes—red, 1½" x 12" (4 x 30.5 cm),
     4 per student

- white tempera paint
- star-shaped stamp

  Styrofoam® "meat" tray

  small wooden blocks

  star pattern (below)

  glue

Steps to Follow

1. Make several star-shaped stamps:
   Use the pattern on this page to trace star shapes onto the
   "meat" tray. Cut out the stars and glue them to small blocks.

2. Place the red strips vertically on the white background,
   making eight even-sized stripes about 1½" (4 cm) wide.

3. Glue blue construction paper across the top.

4. Stamp white-painted stars (nine stars fit nicely) onto the blue field.

**Star
Pattern**

Glittering Fireworks

Brightly colored fireworks explode on the paper and provide motivation for writing a descriptive cinquain verse. The directions for the writing project are on page 10.

Materials

- construction paper—black, 9" x 12" (23 x 30.5 cm)
- white chalk or white colored pencil
- white glue
- cotton swabs
- red, blue, and gold glitter
- containers to pour glitter into

Steps to Follow

1. Fold black paper in half, creasing as lightly as possible.

2. Have students draw shooting fireworks on the top half of the paper. Draw some samples on the chalkboard if students seem to need assistance.

3. Students decide which lines of their fireworks will be gold, which will be red, and which will be blue.

4. Dip a cotton swab into glue and trace over the lines that are going to be one color.

5. Start with one glitter color and pour it over the glue. Let the glitter sit for a minute, then pour off the excess.

6. Repeat steps 4 and 5, using the other two colors of glitter.

7. Set aside the fireworks. Add cinquain verses to the bottom of the page when these are completed.

Hint: Decide in advance how you will organize the glitter application. One possibility is to have separate stations, with adult helpers, for each color. Decide on an orderly method of rotating student through the stations.

Fireworks Cinquain

Cinquain is one of the easier poem styles to use with young students because it does not rhyme. In its "pure" form, cinquain poems have a specific number of syllables in each of the five lines. Here is a simplified form that relies on word count rather than syllables.

Line 1—one word (this will be the title)

Line 2—two words (adjectives that describe the title)

Line 3—three words (decribe an action)

Line 4—four words (describe a feeling about the topic)

Line 5—one word (refers back to the title; a synonym)

Here are some "Fireworks" cinquains:

Fireworks
Colorful, bright
Bursting in air
We all shout "Wow!"
Explosions

Fireworks
Sparkling, glittering
Lighting the sky
What an awesome sight!
Rockets

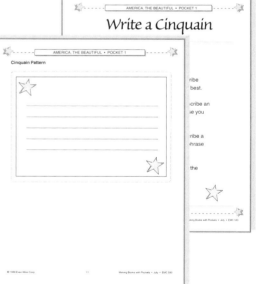

Materials

- five pieces of chart paper, headed Line 1, 2, 3, 4, and 5
- writing form on page 11, reproduced for each student
- cinquain steps on page 12, reproduced on an overhead transparency
- glittering fireworks projects

Steps to Follow

1. Explain to students what a cinquain verse is.
   (a five-line poem that does not rhyme; each line has a certain number of words)

2. Show the overhead transparency and ask students to think about fireworks.

3. Go through each step on the overhead. Brainstorm words and phrases for each of the lines of the verse. List them on the charts.

4. Each student chooses a word or phrase from each list to compose a cinquain verse.

5. Glue the completed writing form to the bottom of the glittering fireworks project.

Cinquain Pattern

Write a Cinquain

Follow these steps:

1. Decide on your one-word title.

2. Think of two-word phrases that describe the title. Choose the phrase you like best.

3. Think of three-word phrases that describe an action of your title. Choose the phrase you like best.

4. Think of four-word phrases that describe a feeling about your title. Choose the phrase you like best.

5. Think of one word that means about the same as your title.

Torn-Paper Star

Hang these stars around the room to celebrate Independence Day. Later put them in Pocket 1 of your America, the Beautiful books.

If your students have not had experience with the torn-paper technique, practice with scrap paper before beginning the project.

> Instruct students to hold the paper between the thumb and forefinger of one hand and to tear with the same fingers of the other hand. As you tear, move the holding fingers along so that they guide the tearing fingers. Practice tearing circles, ovals, and "straight" and curved lines.

Materials

- 12" (30.5 cm) tagboard square
- star pattern on page 14, reproduced for each student
- construction paper
  white, 12" (30.5 cm) square
  blue, 12" (30.5 cm) square
- tissue paper
  two red, 1" x 12" (2.5 x 30.5 cm)
  three white, 1" x 12" (2.5 x 30.5 cm)
- crayons
- glue
- hole punch
- roving, yarn, or twine

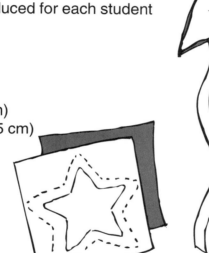

Steps to Follow

1. Cut out the star pattern.

2. Place the star on the tagboard. Trace around it, leaving a border. Cut out the star to make a template.

3. Place the template on the white and blue construction paper and trace around it.

4. Now tear out the two stars.

5. Glue the tissue paper strips along the bottom edge of one star.

6. Glue the two stars together with the tissue sandwiched in between them.

7. Use crayons to draw designs (dots, small stars, dashed lines, etc.) on both sides.

8. Punch a hole in the top point of the star. Tie a loop of roving from which to hang the star.

 Making Books with Pockets • July • EMC 590

Star Pattern

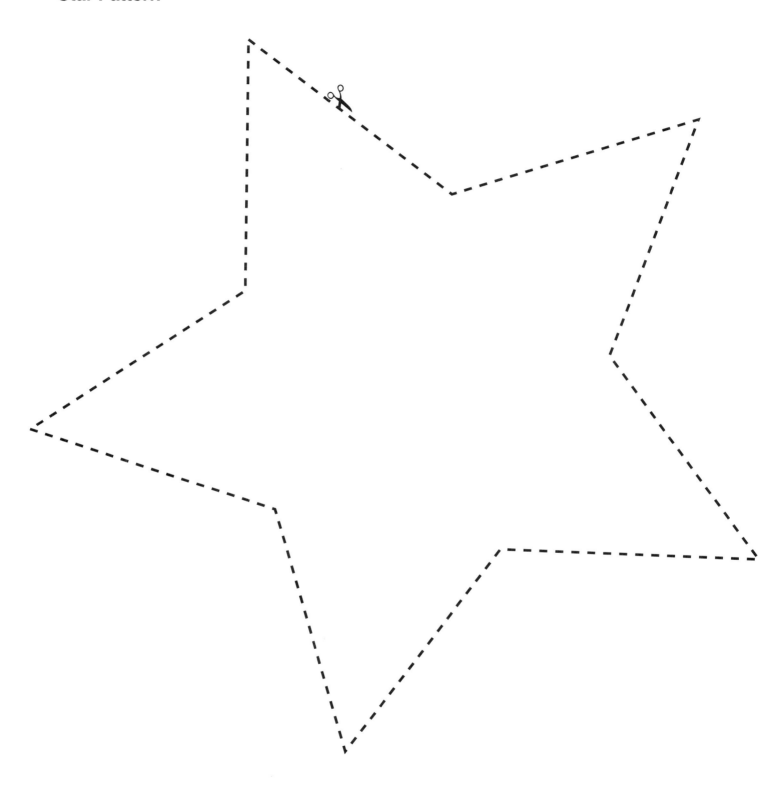

The American Flag
Then and Now

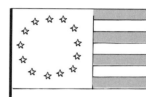

Read *A Flag for Our Country* by Eve Spencer to your class
and talk about the symbols on the American flag and how the
flag has changed over the years.

Materials

- patterns on page 16, reproduced
  on white construction paper for
  each student
- skewer (Cut off the pointed end.)
- glue
- crayons
- scissors

Steps to Follow

1. Color the decorated side of each flag.
   Color the red stripes. Start and finish with an
   outside stripe. Lightly color the blue field so
   that the stars are not covered up.

2. Cut out the flags.

3. Fold one flag around the top part of the skewer
   and glue it closed.

4. Fold the other flag around the bottom part of the
   skewer and glue it closed.

5. On the back of the 13-star flag, write "Then"; on
   the back of the 50-star flag, write "Now."

Patterns for Flags

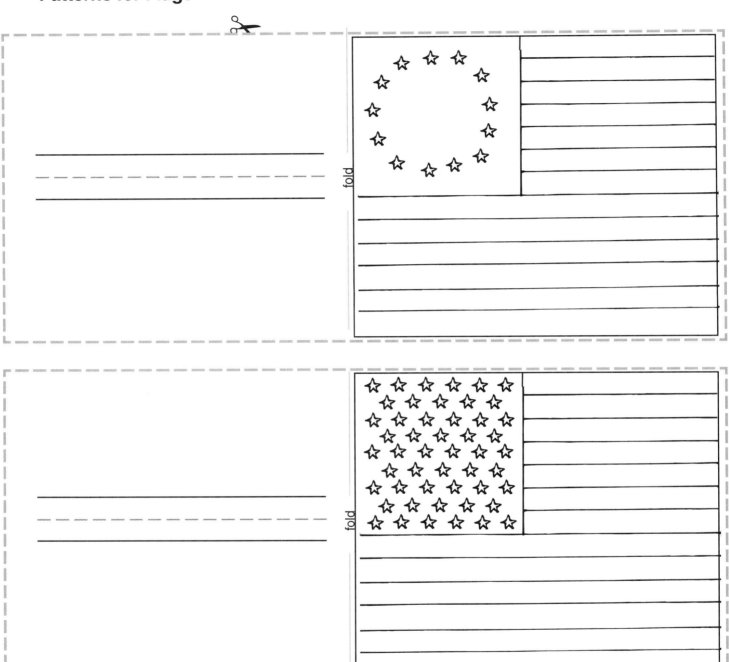

Things Weren't Always Like This

The United States
Then
(1776)

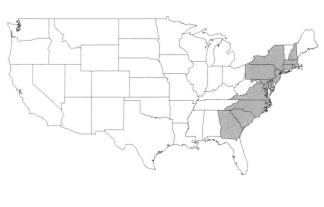

The United States
Now

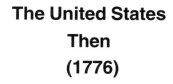

Alaska

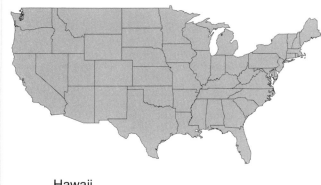

Hawaii

Making Books with Pockets • July • EMC 590

1

When the United States of America became an independent country in 1776, there were just 13 colonies along the Atlantic coast. Now we have 50 states. The last two states are not attached to the main part of the country. The 49th state, Alaska, was added in January, 1959. Hawaii became the 50th state in August, 1959.

Many other things have changed since 1776.

Making Books with Pockets • July • EMC 590

School Then

Long ago, most schoolhouses had just one room. Students of all ages met in that room with one teacher. The older students helped the younger students as they copied their work on slates.

Clothes Then

During the 1800s, women wore many layers of clothes. The large hats were decorated with bows, feathers, ribbons, flowers, and sometimes bird nests!

The men of the 1800s wore pantaloons. These tight pants had straps that fit over the bottoms of the man's boots. The well-dressed man wore a top hat.

Making Books with Pockets • July • EMC 590

Moving Vans Then

When the pioneers of the 1800s moved to new lands in the West, they carried all of their belongings in a big covered wagon. Teams of horses, mules, or oxen pulled the wagons.

The Kitchen Then

The pioneers did most of their cooking in a big pot suspended over a fire in the fireplace. Water was carried into the house in a bucket from a stream or a well. The first refrigerators were called iceboxes because they were big wooden boxes that were cooled by a block of ice.

Making Books with Pockets • July • EMC 590

Draw the way things are now:

School Now

Clothes Now

© 1999 Evan-Moor Corp.　　　Making Books with Pockets • July • EMC 590

Draw the way things are now:

Moving Vans Now

The Kitchen Now

© 1999 Evan-Moor Corp.　　　Making Books with Pockets • July • EMC 590

The Statue of Liberty

Lady Liberty, with the city skyline behind her, beckons to all who enter New York Harbor.

Read about the Statue of Liberty before you do this project. Several good books for young learners are listed in the bibliography on page 5.

Materials

- construction paper
  statue—gray, reproduce pattern on page 22
  background—light blue, 9" x 12" (23 x 30.5 cm)
  water—dark blue, 5" x 9" (13 x 23 cm)
  buildings—black, brown, and purple scraps
  clouds—white scraps
  island—green, 2" x 6" (5 x 15 cm)
     to make statue stand out—2 white, ½" x 2"
     (1.25 x 5 cm) strips

- scissors

- glue

- crayons

- black marker

Steps to Follow

1. Cut out the statue.

2. Cut a wavy edge along one long side of the dark blue paper. Glue it to the bottom of the light blue paper, leaving the wavy edge unglued.

3. Round the green paper to make an island. Glue in the center of the "water."

4. Make buildings from black, brown, and purple scraps. Vary the height and width for interest. Glue the buildings behind the water; then glue the wavy edge of the water down.

5. Using scraps of white paper, cut out clouds and glue them to the sky.

6. Using a black marker, add windows, antennas, and electrical wires.

7. Accordion-fold the two white strips. Glue the end of one strip to the back of the statue's pedestal; glue the other end of that strip to the island.

8. Glue the other folded strip to the back of the statue's shoulders and glue the other end to the background paper.

Statue of Liberty Pattern

Coming to America

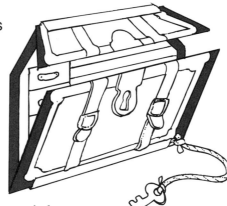

Unless you are a Native American*, your ancestors came to America from somewhere else less than 400 years ago. Help students to understand that the majority of us are descendents of immigrants by reading some of the fine literature listed on page 5. Then present the following lesson that culminates in the recording of family history in a hinged book.

*Note: If you have Native American students, use your computer to prepare an alternate letter and research form so that these students can tell about the history of their tribal group.

Materials

- family history record form on page 24, reproduced for each student
- trunk pattern on page 25, reproduced for each student
- trunk writing form and key pattern on page 26, reproduced for each student
- two pieces of 9" x 12" (23 x 30.5 cm) black construction paper
- 8" (20 cm) piece of yarn
- scrap of yellow posterboard for key
- stapler
- hole punch
- marking pens or crayons
- glue

Steps to Follow

step 3

1. After reading books and discussing how different people came to America, send home the form on page 24 to be filled out with adult assistance.

2. When the forms are returned, have the students transfer the information to the trunk writing forms.

3. Staple the writing forms to one sheet of black construction paper. Trim the edges.

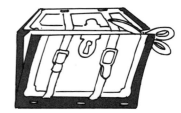

4. Color the trunk pattern. Glue it to the other piece of black construction paper. Trim the edges.

5. Lay the trunk on top of the writing paper. Staple the top and bottom edges.

6. Cut along the line indicated on the trunk.

7. Cut a key from yellow posterboard, using the key pattern. Punch a hole in the key and the corner of the trunk. Tie the key to the trunk with the yarn.

Dear Parents,

In our class we have been reading and talking about the many places Americans have immigrated from throughout the history of this country.

Please help your child fill out information about where one or both sides of your family came from. Return the form to school by _____.

Thank you.

✂ -

Name: _____

Coming to America

Some people in my mother's family came to America from _____.
(name of place)

We think they came in about _____.
(year)

They came here by _____.
(likely means of transportation)

Some people in my father's family came to America from _____.
(name of place)

We think they came in about _____.
(year)

They came here by _____.
(likely means of transportation)

Trunk Pattern

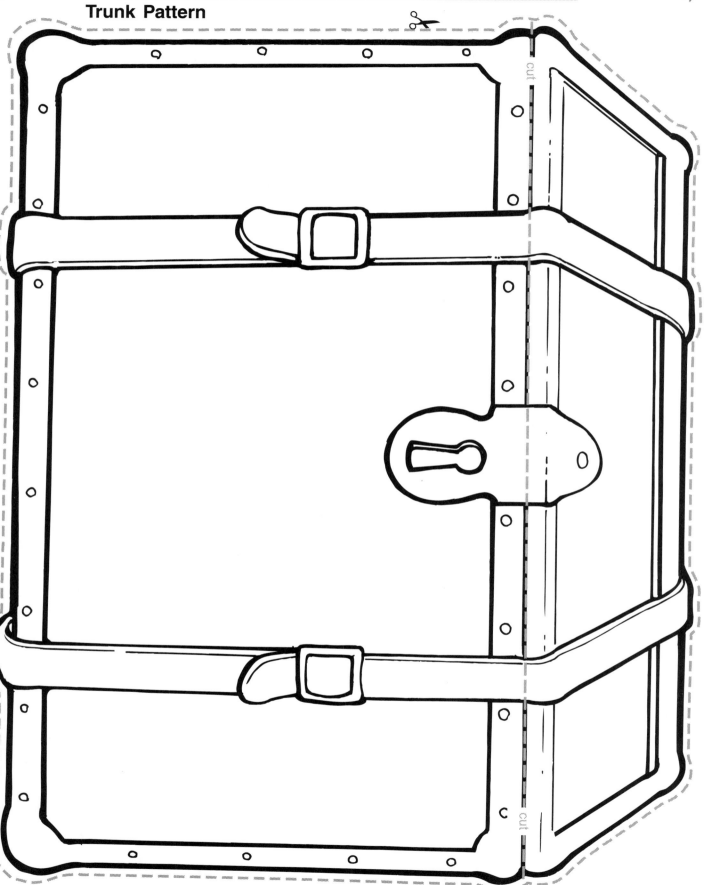

Trunk Writing Form

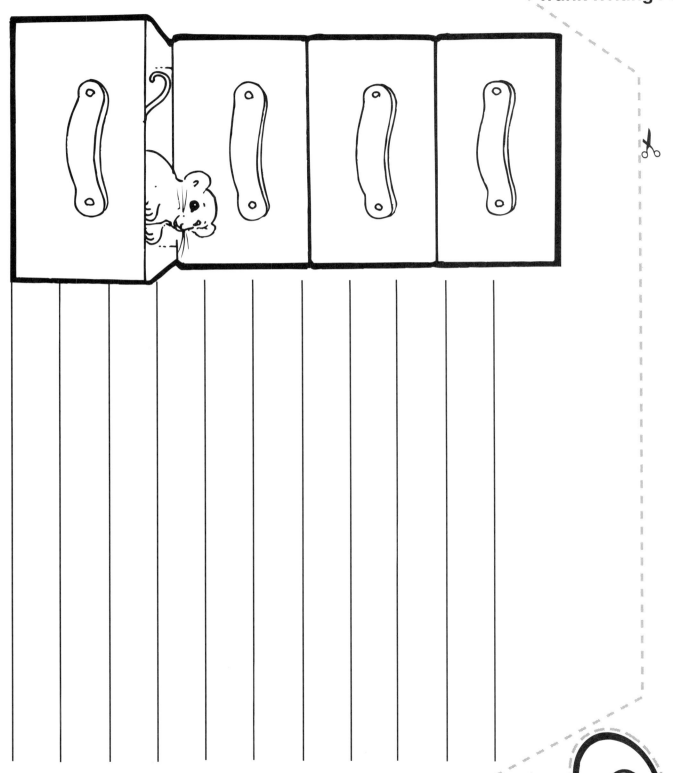

America, the Beautiful Songbook

Your students will be thrilled with the spectacular result of this bookmaking project. Be sure to listen to and sing "America, the Beautiful" before and after you make the book. Take advantage of the opportunity to develop new vocabulary (amber, spacious, majesties, fruited plain, grace, thee) and concepts (How can mountains be purple? Why does the song say "waves of grain"?).

You will probably want to take several sessions to make this book. Provide folders or envelopes in which students may store materials.

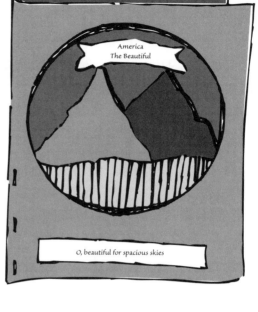

General Materials
- glue
- scissors
- crayons or marking pens

Cover—"O, beautiful for spacious skies"
- 12" x 18" (30.5 x 45.5 cm) dark blue construction paper
- tagboard templates made from the circle pattern on page 29
- patterns on page 30, reproduced for each student

1. Fold dark blue paper in half. Center the circle template on the front cover and trace around it. Cut out the circle.

2. Cut out the first line of the song and glue it on the bottom of the front cover.

3. Cut out the title, "America, the Beautiful," and glue it to the inside of the back cover, with the top corners close to the circle cut-out.

4. Color and cut out the U.S map/flag. Glue it onto the bottom of the inside back cover.

Page 1—"for amber waves of grain"
- 9" x 5" (23 x 13 cm) yellow construction paper
- "amber waves" line of the song from page 30, reproduced for each student

1. Fringe the top edge of the yellow paper.
2. Cut out line 2 of the song and glue it to the yellow paper.

Page 2—"For purple mountain majesties"

- 9" x 8" (23 x 20 cm) dark purple construction paper
- 9" x 8" (23 x 20 cm) light purple construction paper
- tagboard templates made from the mountain pattern on page 31
- "purple mountains" line of the song on page 30, reproduced for each student

1. Trace the mountain template on both pieces of purple construction paper.

2. Tear along the lines that form the points for a jagged mountain peak impression.

3. Glue the light purple mountain in front of the dark purple mountain. You will need to flip one mountain so that there is a straight edge on both sides.

4. Glue the song line to the bottom of the mountains.

Page 3— "above the fruited plain..."

- 9" x 5" (23 x 13 cm) brown construction paper
- pattern on page 32, reproduced for each student

1. Color and cut out the pattern showing the "fruited plain."
2. Glue the pattern to the brown construction paper.

Page 4— "And crown thy good..."

- 9" x 5" (23 x 13 cm) green construction paper
- pattern on page 32, reproduced for each student

1. Color and cut out the pattern showing "brotherhood."
2. Glue the pattern to the green construction paper.

Page 5— "From sea..."

- 9" x 5" (23 x 13 cm) dark blue construction paper
- pattern on page 33, reproduced for each student

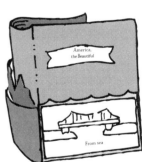

1. Color and cut out the pattern showing the Golden Gate Bridge.
2. Glue the pattern to the blue construction paper.

Page 6— "to shining sea."

- 9" x 5" (23 x 13 cm) turquoise construction paper
- pattern on page 33, reproduced for each student

1. Color and cut out the pattern showing the Statue of Liberty.
2. Glue the pattern to the turquoise construction paper.

Assembling the Book

1. Put all the pages in order, making sure that the left edges are even.
2. Staple the pages inside the cover with the cutout circle on the front.
3. Sing the song as you read along in your beautiful books!

Circle Template for Book Cover

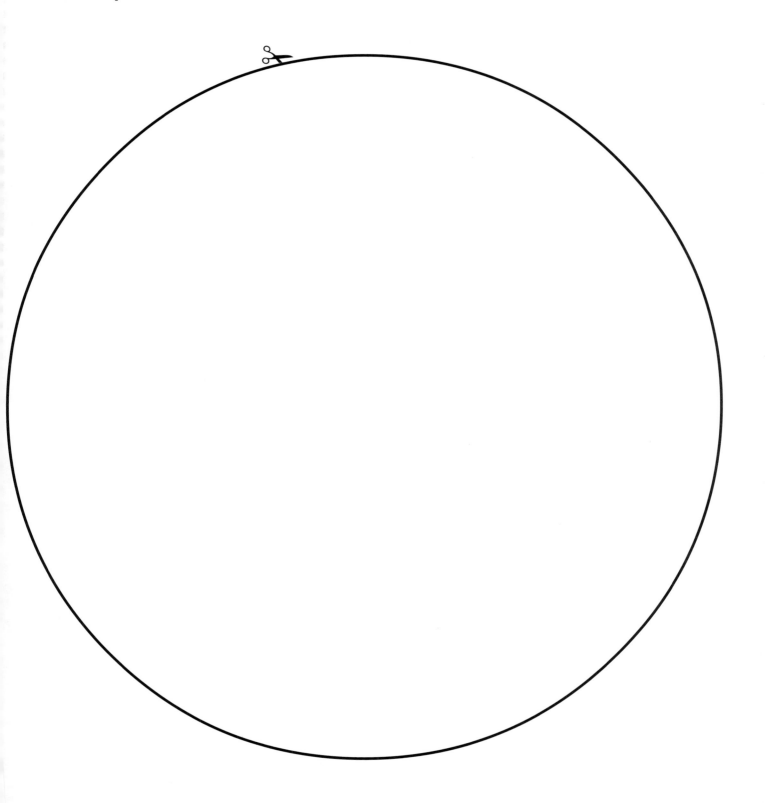

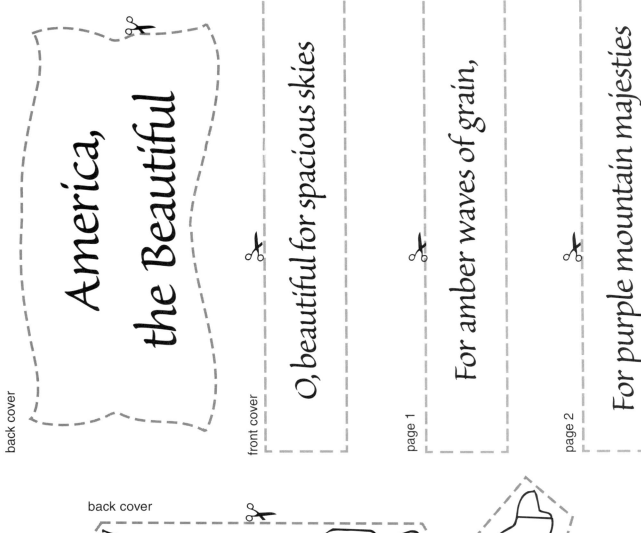

back cover

*America,
the Beautiful*

front cover

O, beautiful for spacious skies

page 1

For amber waves of grain,

page 2

For purple mountain majesties

back cover

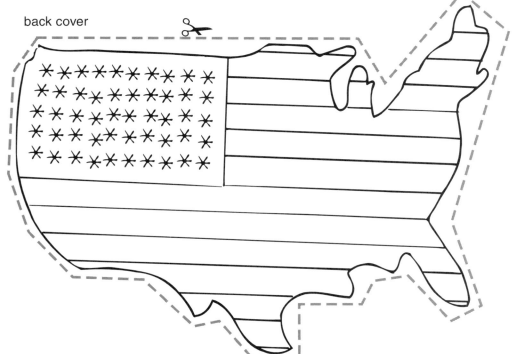

Mountain Template

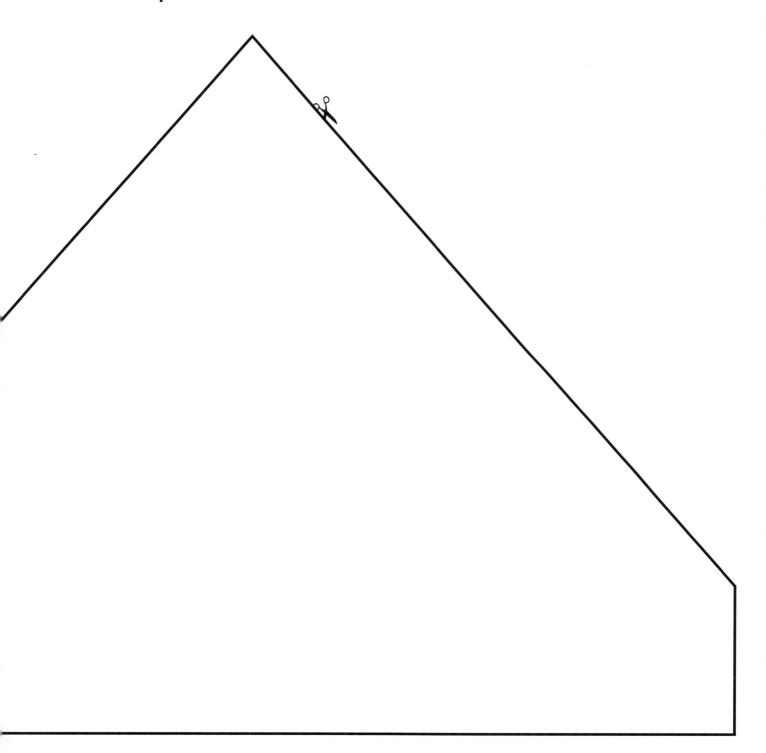

above the fruited plain!
America, America, God shed His grace on thee.

page 3

And crown thy good with brotherhood

page 4

Making Books with Pockets • July • EMC 590

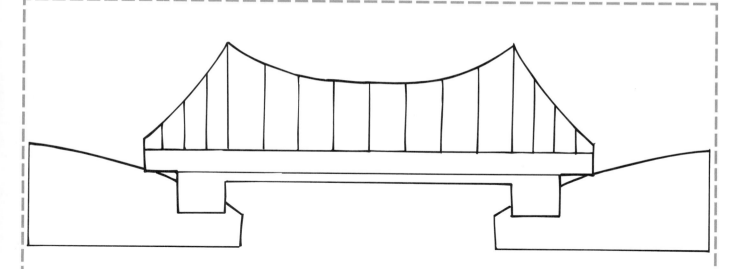

From sea

page 5

to shining sea.

page 6

Note: Reproduce this page and page 35 to label each of the four pockets of the *America* book.

Pocket 1

Fireworks crackle and light up the sky
On Independence Day—the 4th of July.

Pocket 2

Our country has changed. Our flag has, too.
The stars number 50 on the field of blue.

Pocket 3

Immigrants have come from many foreign lands,

Seeking the liberty for which this statue stands.

Pocket 4

Our country now stretches sea to shining sea,

Brimming with abundance for you and for me.

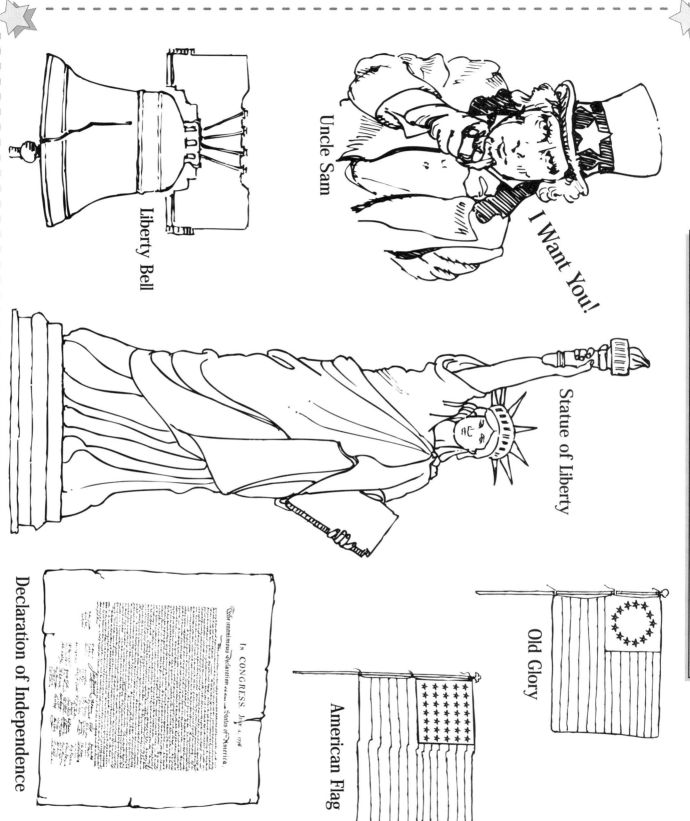

Liberty Bell

Uncle Sam

I Want You!

Statue of Liberty

Old Glory

American Flag

Declaration of Independence

In CONGRESS. July 4, 1776.

Name: _____

Space

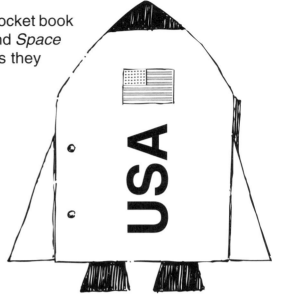

B last off for an adventure in space! The topics in this pocket book include *Our Solar System; Sun, Moon, and Stars;* and *Space Travel.* Students will learn space science information as they write, read a minibook, and create art projects.

Space Book Overview_____ **pages 39 and 40**
These pages show and tell what is in each pocket.

Cover Design_____ **pages 41 and 42**

Pocket Projects _____ **pages 43–61**
Step-by-step directions and patterns for the activities that go in each pocket.

Pocket Labels _____**page 62**

Picture Dictionary _____**page 63**
Use the picture dictionary to introduce new vocabulary and as a spelling reference. Students can add new pictures, labels, and descriptive adjectives to the page as their vocabulary increases.

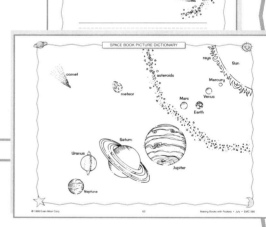

Writing Form _____**page 64**
Use this form for story writing or as a place to record additional vocabulary words.

BIBLIOGRAPHY

Ask Isaac Asimov Series by Isaac Asimov; Gareth Stevens:
    What Is a Shooting Star? 1991
    Why Does the Moon Change Shape? 1991
Astronauts Today by Rosanna Hansen; Random House, 1998.
The Big Dipper by Franklyn M. Branley; HarperCollins, 1991. (Note: Branley's excellent "Let's-Read-and-Find-Out Science Book" series has a number of titles on space. Many are out of print but can be found in libraries.)
Comets, Meteors, and Asteroids by Seymour Simon; William Morrow, 1994.
Energy from the Sun by Allan Fowler; Children's Press, 1998.
Floating in Space by Franklyn M. Branley; HarperCollins, 1998.
The Moon Book by Gail Gibbons; Holiday House, 1998.
The Moon Seems to Change by Franklyn M. Branley; HarperCollins, 1987.
The Planets by Gail Gibbons; Holiday House, 1994.
Our Star: The Sun; Barrons Educational Series, 1993.
The Sun by Seymour Simon; William Morrow, 1986.
The Sun: Our Nearest Star by Franklyn M. Branley, HarperCollins, 1988.

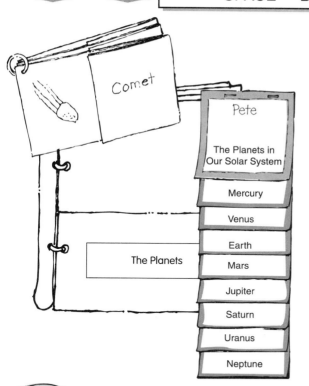

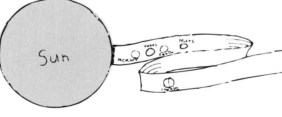

**The Planets in Our
Solar System**   **pages 43–45**
This flip book shows the planets in their order
from the sun and tells some important facts
about each.

How Far from the Sun? pages 46 and 47
Using adding machine tape and cutouts of
the planets, students measure to build a
model of planetary distances from the sun.

**Comets, Asteroids,
and Meteors**   **page 48**
Make a little book on a ring to describe and
draw these space objects.

Sponge-Painted Sun   pages 49 and 50
After creating a bright sponge-painted sun,
students use the form provided to write about
why we need the sun.

**Phases of the
Moon Book**   **pages 51–53**
Cut out a description of each moon phase
and glue it behind the correct flap to make
this informative book.

Stars   **pages 54 and 55**
Students will learn important facts about stars
when they read the minibook they have put
together.

Space Travel

POCKET 3

Humans in Space   **pages 56 and 57**
Color and cut out an astronaut in an MMU and then make the astronaut "move in space."

Rocket to Outer Space   **page 58**
This colorful mitt puppet is fun to make and can be used as a prop in student-created skits.

My Trip to Outer Space   **pages 59–61**
Write an imaginative story and bind it into a rocket-shaped book.

My Trip to Outer Space

Name Paula

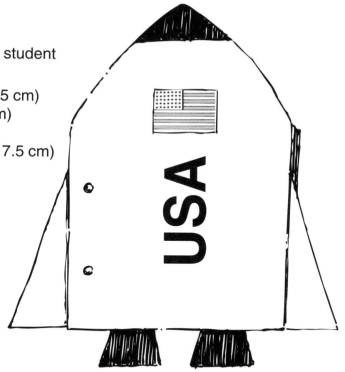

Materials

- patterns on page 42, reproduced for each student
- construction paper
  shuttle body—white, 12" x 18" (30.5 x 45.5 cm)
  shuttle wings—white, 4" x 11" (10 x 28 cm)
  tip of shuttle—black, 3" x 7" (7.5 x 18 cm)
  booster rockets—two black, 3" x 3" (7.5 x 7.5 cm)
- ruler
- scissors
- crayons
- glue
- hole punch
- paper fasteners

Steps to Follow

1. Fold the large white paper lengthwise.

2. Put a pencil mark 6" (15 cm) down from the top. (If your students have not had experience measuring, an adult should do this in advance.)

3. Cut from the pencil mark to the middle of the top to make the nose of the space shuttle.

4. Cut the wing paper in half diagonally. Glue these wings to the sides of the space shuttle.

5. Cut out the letter and flag patterns. Glue them vertically to the center of the shuttle.

6. Glue the large black piece of paper horizontally to the tip of the space shuttle. Trim to the shuttle nose shape.

7. Cut the two smaller pieces of black paper into triangles. Glue them to the backside of the space shuttle.

8. When the book is completed, punch two holes in the left side of the space shuttle and assemble using the paper fasteners.

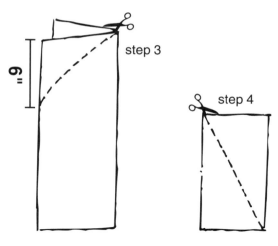

step 3

step 4

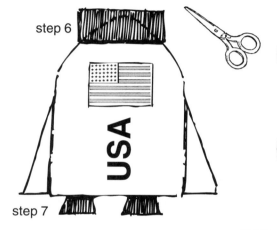

step 6

step 7

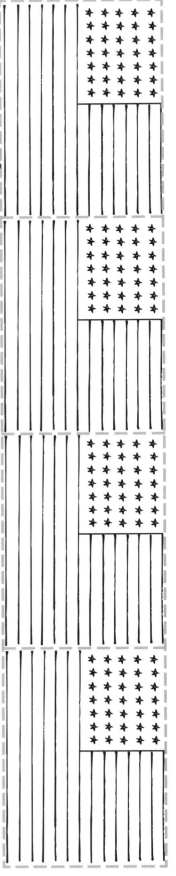

The Planets in Our Solar System

After reading about the planets in our solar system in reference books, use this bookmaking activity to summarize the information students have learned.

Materials

- construction paper for book pages; pages can be all one color or assorted colors
  4" x 16" (10 x 40.6 cm)
  4" x 5" (10 x 13 cm)
  4" x 6" (10 x 15 cm)
  4" x 7" (10 x 18 cm)
  4" x 8" (10 x 20 cm)
  4" x 9" (10 x 23 cm)
  4" x 10" (10 x 25.5 cm)
  4" x 11" (10 x 28 cm)
- patterns on page 44 and 45, reproduced for each student
- crayons, marking pens, or colored pencils
- scissors
- glue
- stapler

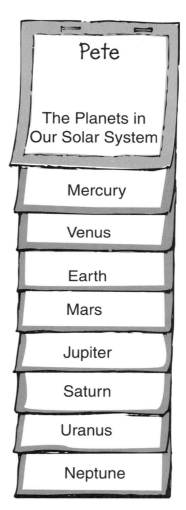

Steps to Follow

1. Fold the 16" (40.6 cm) paper over 4" (10 cm) on one end. This forms the first and last pages of the book.

2. Fit in the remaining seven pages.

3. Staple along the top edge through all pages. (An adult may need to do this.)

4. Read about all the planets on the information sheet.

5. Cut out the information sections and glue them to the pages in planetary order. Align the bottom edges of the information sections with the outside edges of the back pages.

- largest planet
- 16 known moons
- giant ball of gas with a rocky center
- giant red spot may be a storm

Jupiter

- 93 million miles from the sun
- one moon
- has air and water; plants and animals
- has oceans

Earth

- the first planet from the sun
- no moons and no air
- very rocky and dusty with lots of craters
- about 1/3 the size of Earth

Mercury

- second-largest planet
- at least 18 moons
- many rings made of rock and ice
- covered with clouds

Saturn

- about 1/2 the size of Earth
- two moons
- a desert with ice at the poles
- iron in the soil makes it look red

Mars

- almost as big as Earth
- hot and dry with tall mountains and deep valleys
- covered with thick, yellow clouds
- shines low in the western sky at night

Venus

   Making Books with Pockets • July • EMC 590

- a giant ball of gas
- looks blue-green
- tilts over on its side
- has a rock center

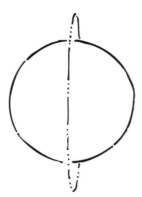

Uranus

- at least eight moons
- covered with clouds
- very, very cold
- high winds and many storms

Neptune

Name:

_____

The Planets in Our Solar System

45

How Far from the Sun?

This model will give students an idea of the relative distances that the planets are from the sun. If your students are new to measuring, you may want to do step 4 in small groups with adult assistance.

Materials

- 6" (15 cm) square of yellow construction paper
- 7' (2.2 m) strip of adding machine tape
- planet patterns on page 47, reproduced for each student
- a lid or small box to hold the cutout planets until they are glued
- marking pen
- ruler
- glue

Steps to Follow

1. Round the edges of the yellow paper to form a circle. Write "Sun" on the circle with the marking pen.

2. Glue the adding machine tape to the back of the sun.

3. Color and cut out the planets. Put them in the container to keep them from being misplaced.

4. Measure distances and glue the planets to the tape. Measure Mercury from the outside edge of the sun; measure the remaining planets from the outside edge of the previous planet.

Mercury	1" (2.5 cm)			
Venus	½" (1.25 cm)		**Saturn**	7½" (19.25 cm)
Earth	½" (1.25 cm)		**Uranus**	19" (48.25 cm)
Mars	1" (2.5 cm)		**Neptune**	22" (56 cm)
Jupiter	8½" (21.25 cm)			

5. Fold or roll the tape and paper clip to the sun for storage in the pocket.

Planet Patterns

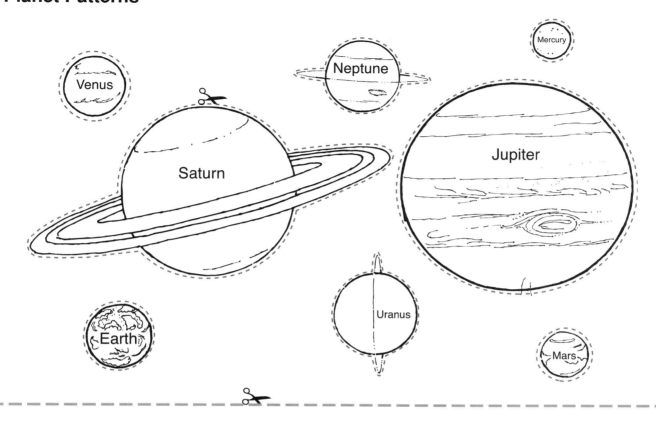

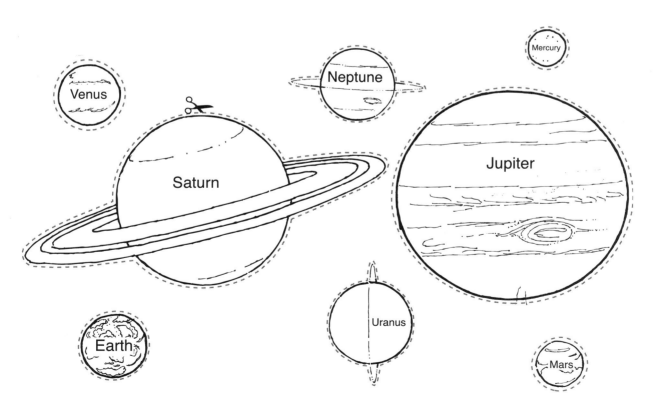

Comets, Asteroids, and Meteors
Little Book on a Ring

Read information in books such as *Comets, Meteors, and Asteroids* by Seymour Simon. Record what students remember on charts that they can refer to when writing their books.

Materials

- three pieces of white construction paper, 4 ½" x 12" (11.5 x 30.5 cm)
- ruler
- pencil
- marking pens
- scissors
- hole punch
- small loose leaf ring or paper fastener

Steps to Follow

1. Fold over 4" (10 cm) on one end of each white paper.

2. Create a page for each word—Comet, Asteroid, Meteor—as shown.

3. Punch a hole in the top left corner of each paper and assemble the three pages using a loose leaf ring or a paper fastener.

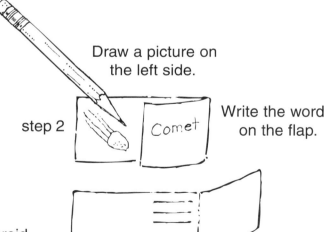

Draw a picture on the left side.

step 2

Write the word on the flap.

Open the flap and write about the object.

Sponge-Painted Sun

On the back of this cheerful sun you can mount the writing project described below.

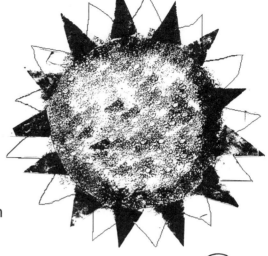

Materials

- 12" (30.5 cm) square of white construction paper
- orange and yellow tissue paper, cut into triangles about 2" (5 cm) high by 1" (2.5 cm) wide—about 25 per student
- 7" (18 cm) tagboard circles
- writing form on page 50, reproduced for each student
- orange and yellow tempera paints
- flat containers for paint
- sponges cut into 1" (2.5 cm) pieces
- newspaper to cover work areas
- liquid starch
- pencil
- paintbrush

Steps to Follow

1. Center the circle template on the white paper and trace around it.

2. Sponge paint inside the circle, overlapping the two colors of paint.

3. After the paint is dry, brush starch in a wide band around the perimeter of the circle.

4. Lay the tissue paper triangles around the circle. Alternate orange and yellow, and slightly overlap the bases.

5. Paint over the tissue paper with starch to secure the triangles.

6. When the starch is dry, cut around the triangles to create a "sun."

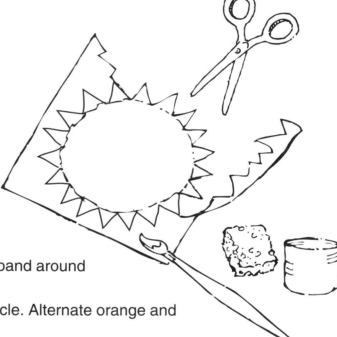

Writing Project

Read about how the sun helps us in books such as *Energy from the Sun* by Allan Fowler. List as many ideas as your students generate about why we need the sun.

Then have each student write three reasons why we need the sun on the sun writing form.

Cut out the writing form and glue it to the back of the sponge-painted sun.

Sun Writing Form

Why We Need the Sun

Name: _____

1. _____

_____

2. _____

_____

3. _____

_____

Phases of the Moon Book

Using books that are appropriate to the level of your students, read about how the moon seems to change shape. As you guide students through this project, read and discuss the information about each phase before students glue the information behind the correct flap.

Materials

- construction paper
  book—black, 12" x 18" (30.5 x 45.5 cm)
  moon phases—yellow, 2" (5 cm) squares,
    4 per student
  new moon—black, 2" (5 cm) square, 1 per student
- information on page 53, reproduced
  for each student
- white colored pencil
- pencil
- scissors
- glue

Steps to Follow

Make the book:

1. Fold black construction paper in half crosswise. Fold in half two more times, making a total of eight sections.

2. Open up the paper and fold in half lengthwise.

3. Cut along each crease of the top section only, creating a flap. You will have eight flaps.

4. Turn the paper so that the fold is on the left. Using a white colored pencil, write one moon phase on the bottom left side of each flap, as shown in the illustration.

new

its orbit around the Earth.
a small part of the moon.

first quarter

waxing gibbous

full

waning gibbous

last quarter

crescent

Make the moon phases:

Have students make circles by rounding the corners of the four yellow squares and the black square. As you do the steps below, ask questions to help students decide on which flap each piece should be placed.

1. "Why is one circle black? Where should we paste this circle?" (This is the "new moon.")

2. Paste a yellow circle to the "full" flap.

3. Cut a yellow circle in half. Glue one of the halves to the "first quarter" flap and the other half to the "last quarter" flap.

last quarter   first quarter

4. On each of the two remaining circles, draw a line to form a crescent. It should be about a fourth of the surface of the circle. Cut off the two crescents, and glue them to the flaps as shown.

top crescent flap

bottom crescent flap

5. The pieces remaining make the waxing and waning gibbous moons. Glue them to the flaps as shown.

waxing gibbous

waning gibbous

Add the information sections:

1. Direct students to cut off a specific information section.

2. Read the information together and decide under which flap it should be glued.

3. Repeat with each remaining section.

The sun shines on the backside of the moon. The side that faces Earth is in the dark. **new**	All of the side facing the Earth is now lit. **full**
The moon has moved in its orbit around the Earth. Now the sun shines on a small part of the moon. **crescent**	The moon seems to be getting smaller. Three-fourths of the moon's surface is now lit. **waning gibbous**
The moon has moved around the first quarter of its orbit. The sun lights half of the side facing us. **first quarter**	The moon is on the last quarter of its orbit. The sun lights half of the side facing us. **last quarter**
The moon seems to be growing. Three-fourths of the moon's surface is now lit. **waxing gibbous**	The amount of lighted moon that we see is getting still smaller. In a few days, there will be another new moon. **crescent**

All of the side facing the Earth is now lit.

The moon seems to be getting smaller. Three-fourths of the moon's surface is now lit.

The moon is on the last quarter of its orbit. The sun lights half of the side facing us.

The amount of lighted moon that we see is getting still smaller. In a few days, there will be another new moon.

The sun shines on the backside of the moon. The side that faces Earth is in the dark.

The moon has moved in its orbit around the Earth. Now the sun shines on a small part of the moon.

The moon has moved around the first quarter of its orbit. The sun lights half of the side facing us.

The moon seems to be growing. Three-fourths of the moon's surface is now lit.

Stars

Stars are huge balls of hot gases. The hot gases give off heat and light. We can feel the heat from our special star, the sun. Other stars are so far away that we cannot feel their heat.

Stars are always in the sky, even during the daytime. We can't see them because our sun makes so much light that the other stars are hidden. At night, when our part of the Earth turns away from the sun, we can see the other stars.

Making Books with Pockets • July • EMC 590

There are billions of stars in the sky. You can see about 2,000 stars without binoculars or a telescope. Stars seem to twinkle. That's because the air around the Earth bends the light from the stars.

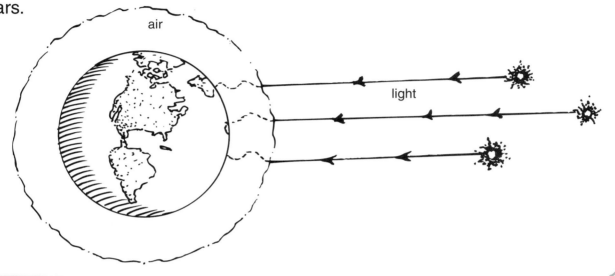

air

light

Making Books with Pockets • July • EMC 590

Groups of stars are called constellations. Long ago, people thought these groups of stars looked like objects and gave them names.

The Fish (Pisces)   The Hunter (Orion)

Making Books with Pockets • July • EMC 590

Humans in Space

Read about astronauts and cosmonauts in resources that are appropriate to the level of your students. Make sure you are using recent resources that mention the Mir space station and recent space shuttle missions. In the art project below, students will make an astronaut in an MMU (manned maneuvering unit). For the project to be meaningful, it is important that students understand what an MMU is.

Materials

- patterns on page 57, reproduced for each student
- 9" x 12" (23 x 30.5 cm) black construction paper
- gold stars, 4 or 5 per student
- mat knife (for teacher's use)
- crayons or marking pens
- scissors
- glue
- small paper fastener

Steps to Follow

1. In advance of the project, you will need to cut a line on the black construction paper as shown.

2. Direct students to color and cut out the "Earth" and the astronaut in the MMU. Also cut out the backing circle.

3. Glue the "Earth" to the bottom of the black paper. (Make sure that students have oriented the black paper correctly before gluing.)

4. Push the paper fastener through the black dot on the astronaut. Put the fastener through the slit in the black paper. Put the backing circle behind the black paper and push the fastener through the center of the circle. Open the fastener. Now your astronaut can maneuver in space!

5. Stick the stars on the background to add an outer space feel.

6. Have students write a statement on the lines about the MMU.

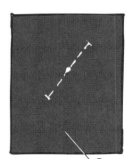

Save room for the Earth.

backside

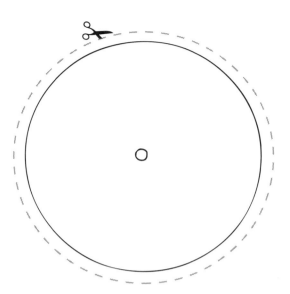

backing circle

astronaut

Earth

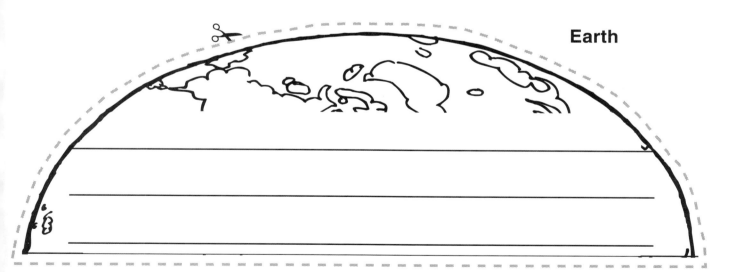

Rocket to Outer Space
A Mitt Puppet

After making these spiffy rockets,
use them as props for student-created
skits about a trip to space.

Materials

- rocket body—silver foil wrapping paper
  9" x 12" (23 x 30.5 cm)
- construction paper
  rocket nose—red, 6" x 9" (15 x 23 cm)
  rocket fins—blue, 3" x 4" (7.5 x 10 cm)
- red, orange, and yellow tissue paper
- glue
- scissors
- black marker

Steps to Follow

1. Fold the foil paper for the rocket body. Glue two edges shut.

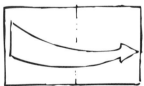

2. Make the rocket nose by cutting the red paper as shown. Use
   the large triangle for the front and put the two smaller triangles
   together for the backside. Glue the pieces to the rocket body.

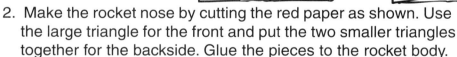

3. Cut the blue paper for the rocket
   fins. Glue them to the rocket body.

4. Cut flames from the tissue paper and glue them inside one side of the mitt.

5. With a black marker, add details to create an original rocket.

Making Books with Pockets • July • EMC 590

My Trip to Outer Space

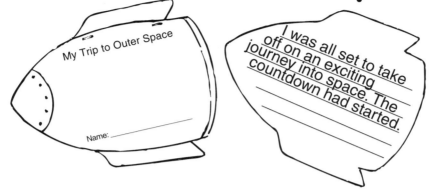

My Trip to Outer Space

Name: _____

I was all set to take off on an exciting journey into space. The countdown had started.

Now that students have learned about the solar system, the moon and stars, and a bit about astronauts, they have the background to be able to write creatively about a journey into space.

Before writing, discuss what students remember about space flight. On a large chart, create a word bank of words that students may want to use in their stories.

Reproduce the book cover on page 60 and multiple copies of the writing form on page 61 for each student.

Revise, Rewrite, and Edit

Students will be anxious to share their completed stories. Use this motivation to encourage students to revise and rewrite. If you decide to work through this process, have students write their stories on regular writing paper before copying them onto the writing forms.

1. Talk with the class about elements that make a story fun to read. List these elements on a chart.

   • The story makes sense.

     • The story has a beginning—You meet the main characters and get an idea of what the story is going to be about.

     • The story has a middle—There is a problem or something interesting happens.

     • The story has an ending—The problem is solved; your questions are answered.

     • There are vivid words to describe things and actions.

2. Have pairs of students share their stories and give each other suggestions using the ideas on the chart. Students then revise and rewrite their stories.

3. Form new pairs of students and have them work together to edit both stories. Before making these assignments, establish benchmarks that are appropriate for the level of your students. For example, it may be reasonable for some third-grade students to use quotation marks. Beginning writers may have the single goal of using periods correctly.

4. Copy the edited stories onto the writing forms. Cut out the forms and the cover and staple the stories together.

5. Allow students to share their stories with the class.

Book Cover

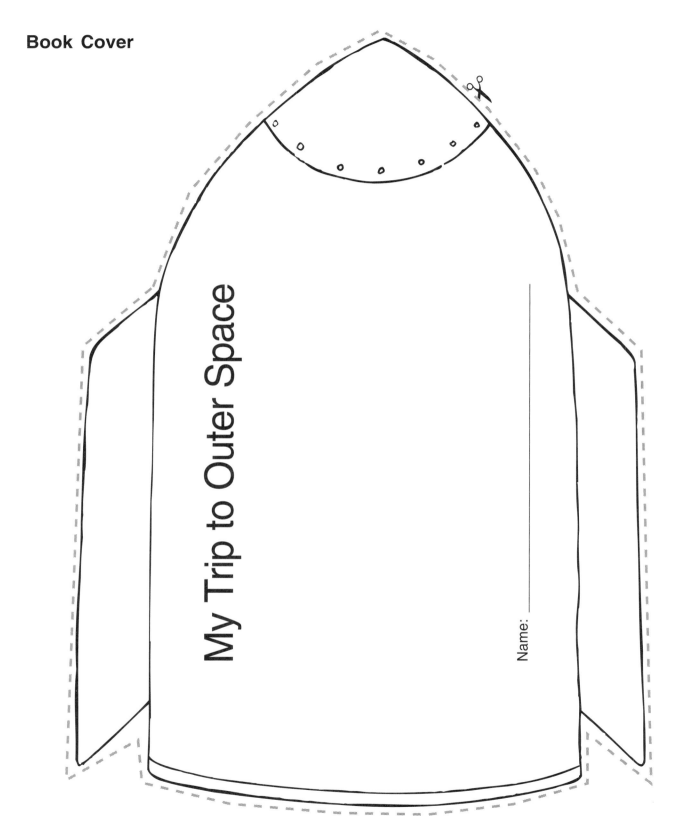

My Trip to Outer Space

Name:

Writing Form

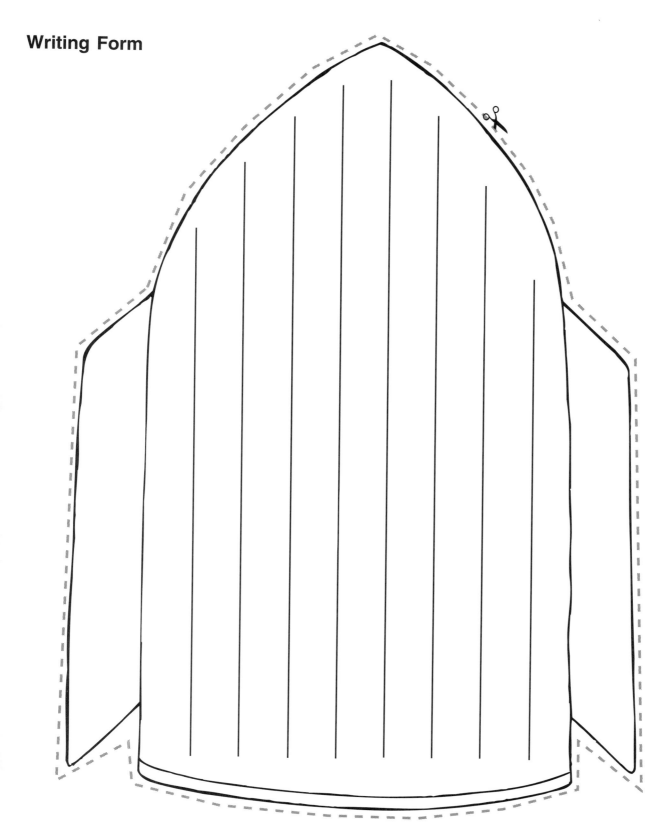

Note: Reproduce this page to label each of the three pockets of the Space Book.

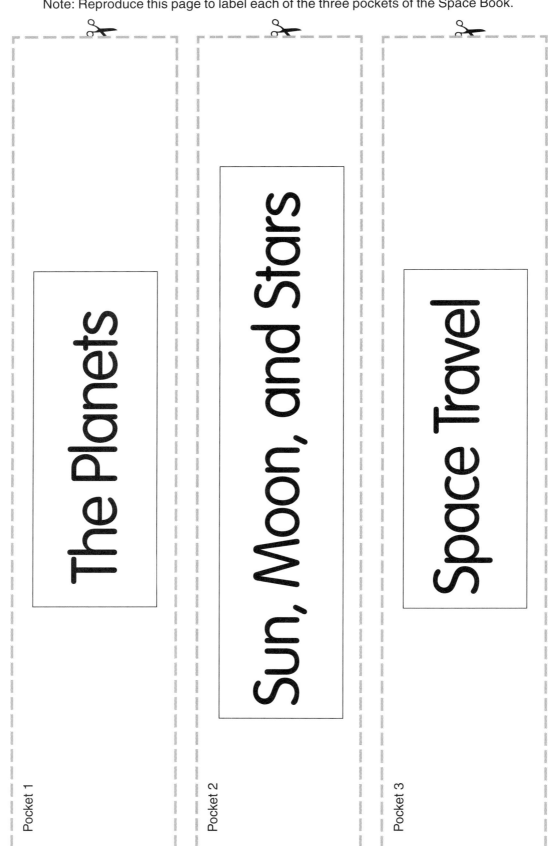

The Planets

Pocket 1

Sun, Moon, and Stars

Pocket 2

Space Travel

Pocket 3

SPACE PICTURE DICTIONARY

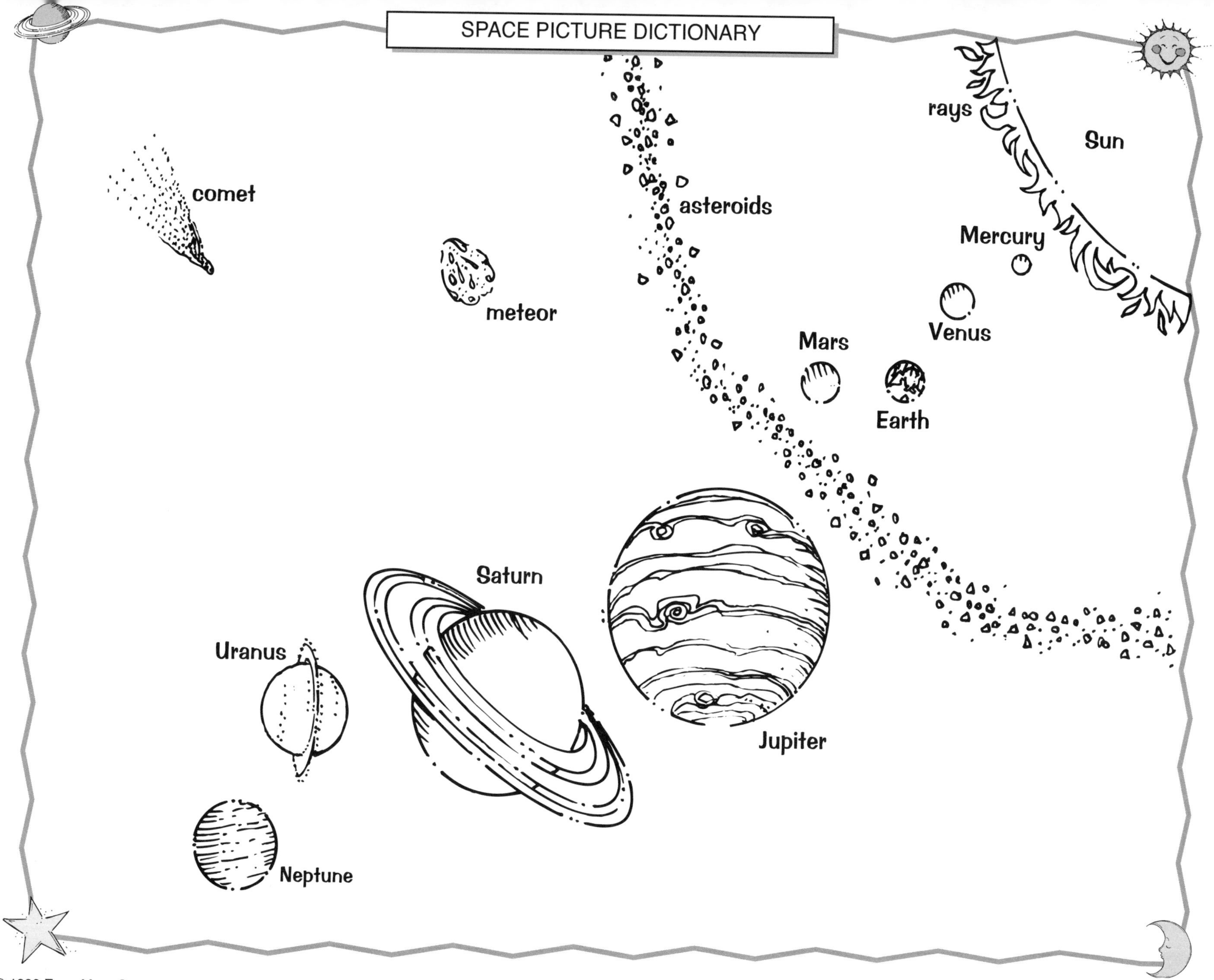

Sun

rays

Mercury

Venus

Earth

Mars

asteroids

Jupiter

meteor

Saturn

comet

Uranus

Neptune

Making Books with Pockets • July • EMC 590

Name: _____

Transportation

We live in a world on the move—people and goods travel far and wide. The art and writing projects in this pocket book will help children learn about transportation in the air, on land, and in the water.

**Transportation
Book Overview** _____ **pages 66 and 67**
These pages show and tell what is in each pocket.

Cover Design _____ **pages 68 and 69**

Pocket Projects _____ **pages 70–88**
Step-by-step directions and patterns for the activities that go in each pocket.

Pocket Labels _____ **page 89**

Picture Dictionary _____ **page 90**
Use the picture dictionary to introduce new vocabulary and as a spelling reference. Students can add new pictures, labels, and descriptive adjectives to the page as their vocabulary increases.

Writing Form _____ **page 91**
Use this form for story writing or as a place to record additional vocabulary words.

BIBLIOGRAPHY

The Airplane Alphabet Book by Jerry Pallotta; Charlesbridge, 1997.
On the Go by Ann Morris; Mulberry Books, 1994.
On the Move by Henry Pluckrose; Franklin Watts, 1998.
Some Planes Hover (I Didn't Know That) by Kate Petty; Cooper Beech Books, 1998.
Wings, Wheels, & Sails by Bobbie Kalman; Crabtree, 1995.
Books by Donald Crews: *Flying, Freight Train, Rockets, Truck*
Books by Gail Gibbons: *Bicycle Book, Boat Book, Trains, Trucks*
Books by Darlene Stille: *Airplanes, Blimps, Helicopters, Spacecraft, Trains, Trucks*
Usborne Books: *Planes and Helicopters, Tractors, Trucks*

POCKET 1

Make a Helicopter
Spinner   pages 70 and 71
This fun, hands-on activity will give students an idea about how helicopters work.

How Does It Fly?   pages 72–75
Modify a basic paper airplane, test it to see how it flies, and record your results on a "Flight Test Record Sheet."

Up, Up, and Away   page 76
Students answer air transportation riddles by pasting a picture answer next to the riddle.

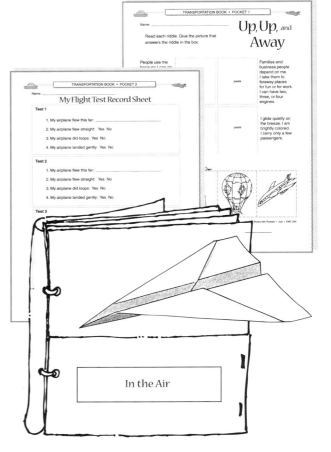

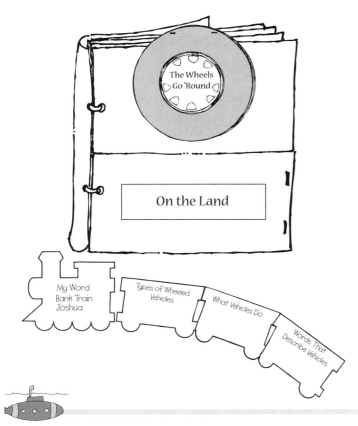

POCKET 2

Before beginning Pocket 2, gather resources about many forms of transportation with wheels. If possible, locate books that your students can read independently. Share information about a number of kinds of vehicles.

Word Bank Trains   pages 77 and 78
These colorful accordion-folded trains carry all types of words that students will use in writing about wheeled vehicles.

The Wheels Go 'Round   pages 79–82
Individual students or small groups choose a wheeled vehicle and write a report on the forms provided.

POCKET 3

Sailboat Shape Poems   **pages 83–85**
Words and phrases about sailboats form the sail of this sailboat.

Submarine Shape Book   **pages 86–88**
Gather words that begin with *sub* or *under* and write them on the pages of this book shaped like a submarine.

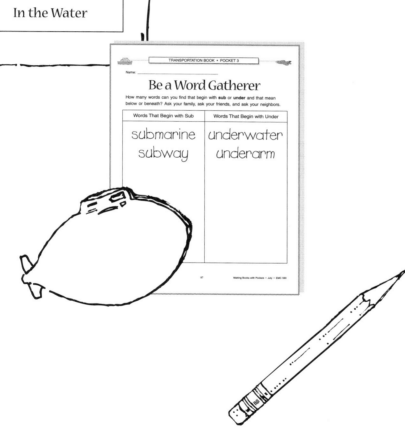

Head off to explore the world of transportation in this personalized bus. Students can draw or add a photograph of themselves in the bus. Give the bus a name—student's name, school name, etc.

Materials

- construction paper
  bus—yellow, 12" (30.5 cm) square
  windshield—white, 10" x 4" (25.5 x 10 cm)
  bumper—gray, 2" x 14" (5 x 35.5 cm)
  wheels—black, 2" x 4" (5 x 10 cm),
    2 per student

- patterns on page 69, reproduced on white construction paper for each student

- glue

- scissors

- crayons or marking pens

Steps to Follow

1. Round the upper corners of the yellow paper. Note: You will want to round the other pockets as well before putting the book together.

2. Round the top corners of the "windshield" and glue near the top of the yellow paper.

3. Round the ends of the gray "bumper" and glue it near the bottom of the yellow paper.

4. Round both ends of the wheels. Glue them on the backside of the "bus," with about ½ of the wheel showing in front.

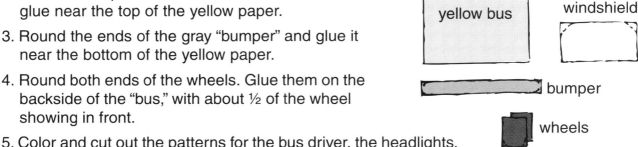

yellow bus   windshield

bumper

wheels

5. Color and cut out the patterns for the bus driver, the headlights, and the grill. Glue them to the bus.

6. Add the desired name to the bus sign, cut it out, and glue it to the top of the bus.

7. If desired, students may draw themselves on the bus—or glue on a photograph.

Bus Patterns

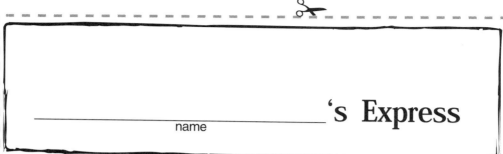

_____ 's Express
name

driver

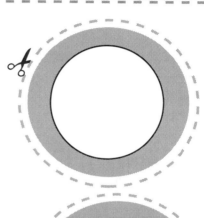

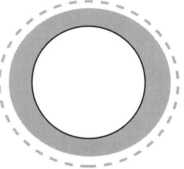

headlights

grill

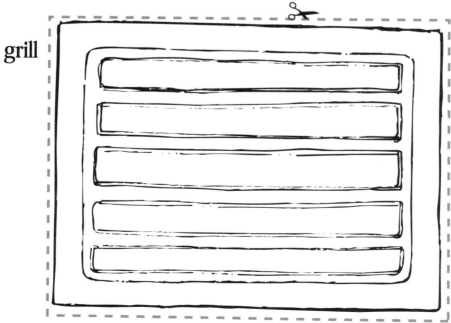

Make a Helicopter Spinner

After reading books about helicopters, use this fun activity to give students an idea about how helicopters work.

Students will see that as gravity pulls the spinner toward the ground, the spinner's fall is slowed—and the blades spun—by resistance (friction) between the paper and the air.

Challenge students to make one change in the design of the helicopter (i.e., changing the direction of the rotor, adding paper clips, etc.) and then test it to see how the change affects the motion.

Materials

- pattern on page 71, reproduced for each student
- scissors
- crayons

Steps to Follow

1. Color and cut out the pattern.

2. Fold as indicated on the pattern.

3. Allow students to drop the spinner by standing on a tabletop. (Make sure you have some adult spotters available!)

Helicopter Spinner Pattern

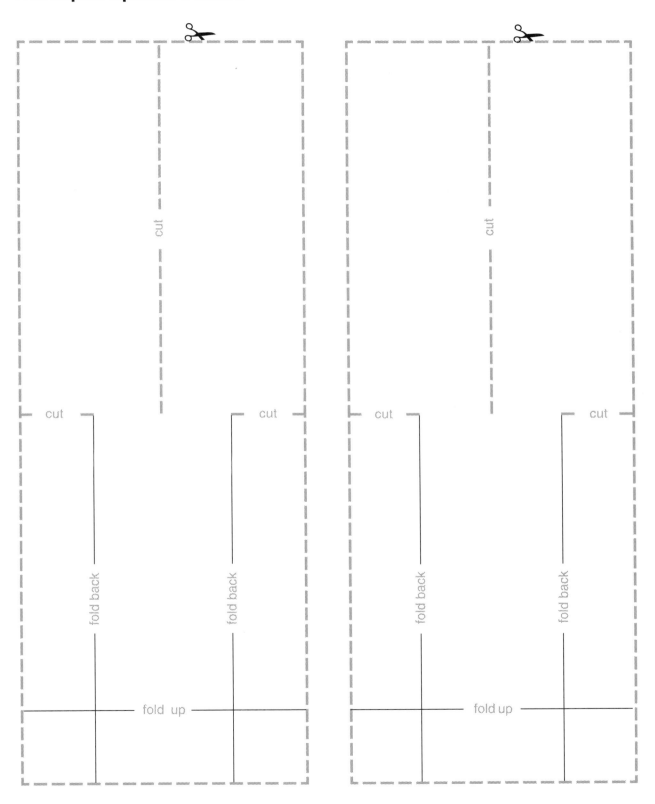

How Does It Fly?

Read from books that explain airplanes in simple terms. Conduct the following demonstration. Then, let students make their own paper airplanes, fly them, and record the "flight" results.

Teacher Demonstration

1. Hold a piece of copy paper by the top edges with your thumb and index finger. Place your middle fingers a little farther down the paper so that you are lifting up the first few inches of the paper. The remainder will hang down.

2. Tell students that you are going to show them something that will give them a clue about how airplanes are able to fly. Say, "I am going to blow across the top of this paper. What do you think will happen?" Allow time for responses.

3. Blow across the top of the section of paper that you are lifting up. (The paper will lift up.)

4. Explain that this is how airplane wings work. The air going over the bulge on the top of the wing has to go faster than the air going under the wing, The faster moving air does not push down as hard as the slower moving air pushes up, so the wing is lifted up.

Materials

- several sheets of copy paper for each student
- overhead transparency of basic airplane directions on page 74
- record sheet on page 75, reproduced for each student
- "clipboards" made from cardboard with a pencil attached
- yardsticks, metersticks, or tape measures

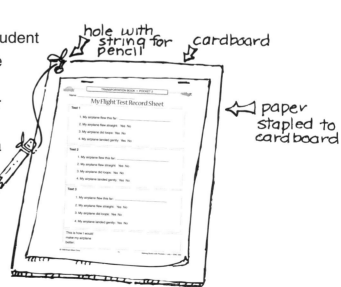

hole with string for pencil   cardboard

paper stapled to cardboard

Steps to Follow

1. Guide students through the steps to make a paper airplane as shown on page 74.

2. Divide students into small groups and experiment with flying the airplanes.

3. Talk about how students might make changes to their airplanes to improve flight. Have a number of basic airplanes made up so that you can demonstrate some of the ideas for modification shown on the bottom of this page.

4. Have students make a second airplane and make one or two modifications to it.

5. Explain the record sheet.

6. Take students to a large area where they can fly their airplanes and record the results of the "flight tests." Have a number of adults or cross-age tutors available to help with measuring.

Sample Modifications (See step 3 above)

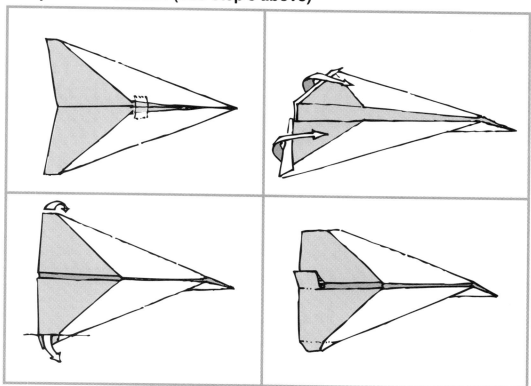

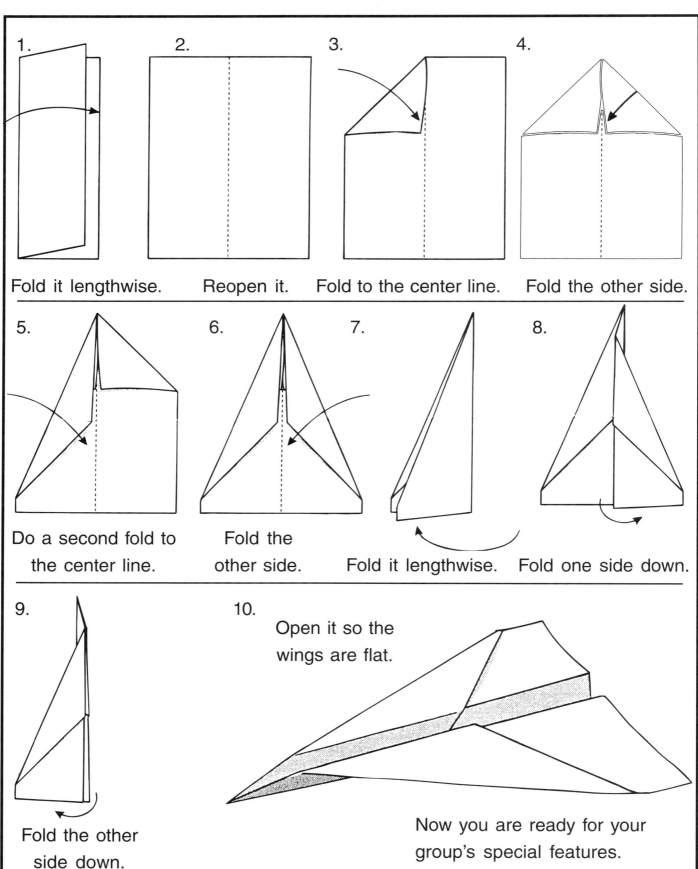

1. Fold it lengthwise.

2. Reopen it.

3. Fold to the center line.

4. Fold the other side.

5. Do a second fold to the center line.

6. Fold the other side.

7. Fold it lengthwise.

8. Fold one side down.

9. Fold the other side down.

10. Open it so the wings are flat.

Now you are ready for your group's special features.

Name: _____

My Flight Test Record Sheet

Test 1

    1. My airplane flew this far: _____

    2. My airplane flew straight: Yes No

    3. My airplane did loops: Yes No

    4. My airplane landed gently: Yes No

Test 2

    1. My airplane flew this far: _____

    2. My airplane flew straight: Yes No

    3. My airplane did loops: Yes No

    4. My airplane landed gently: Yes No

Test 3

    1. My airplane flew this far: _____

    2. My airplane flew straight: Yes No

    3. My airplane did loops: Yes No

    4. My airplane landed gently: Yes No

This is how I would make my airplane better:

Name: _____

Read each riddle. Glue the picture that answers the riddle in that box.

Up, Up, and Away

People use me because I can go straight up and down. I can land in small spaces. Emergency workers depend on me.

paste

paste

Families and business people depend on me. I take them to faraway places for fun or for work. I can have two, three, or four engines.

Only a few people ever get to ride in me. I zoom far away from the Earth. Some day, I may take people to other planets.

paste

paste

I glide quietly on the breeze. I am brightly colored. I carry only a few passengers.

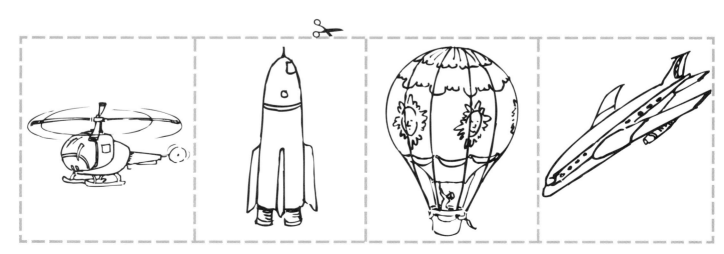

Making Books with Pockets • July • EMC 590

Word Bank Trains

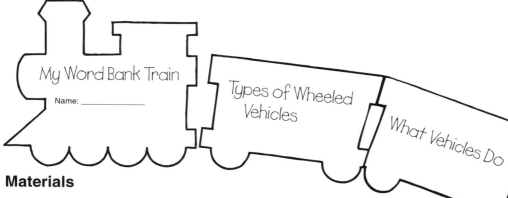

My Word Bank Train

Name: _____

Types of Wheeled Vehicles

What Vehicles Do

Words That Describe Vehicles

Materials

- tagboard templates of train engine and train car on page 78
- construction paper
  engine—red, 8" (20 cm) square
  cars—yellow, 4" x 18" (10 x 45.5 cm)
- scissors
- crayons
- cellophane tape
- pencil

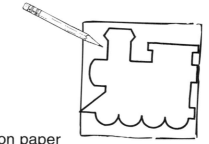

Steps to Follow

1. Trace the engine template onto the red construction paper and cut it out. Color the smokestack and wheels black.

2. Fold the yellow paper in thirds. The sections need to be equal or the template for the train car will not fit. (Younger students will need help to do this.)

3. Place the train car template on the folded paper and trace around it. Cut out the shape. Do not cut the fold.

4. Tape the first car to the back of the engine.

Making a Word Bank

1. Have students write a title on the engine and each of the cars.

2. Brainstorm and list words and phrases in the three categories. Have the students copy words onto the cars in their word trains.

3. Stand the train on the desk to use as a reference for writing. Add the word train to Pocket 2 at the end of your study of land transportation.

Templates for Engine and Cars

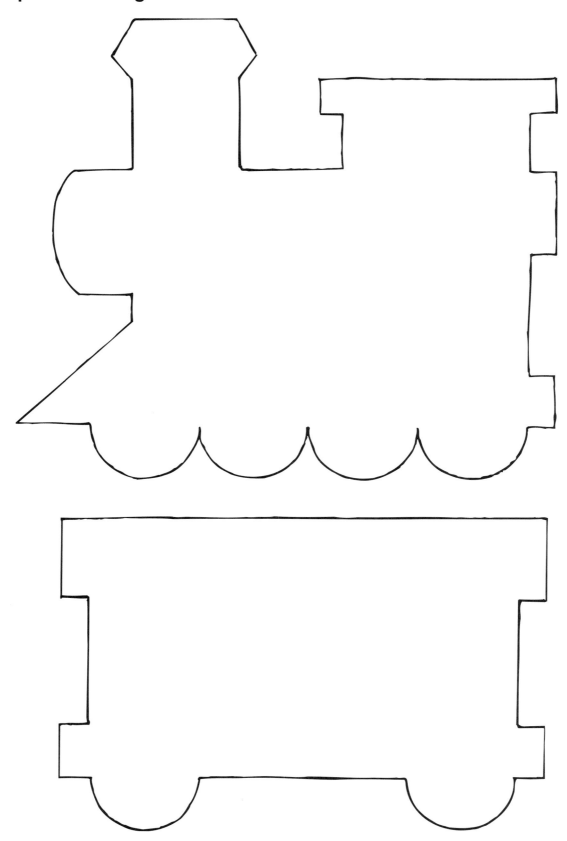

The Wheels Go 'Round
A Vehicle Report

Before beginning the activities in this pocket, you gathered multiple resources on wheeled vehicles. Students will use these to gather information for their individual reports.

Materials

- book cover pattern on page 80, reproduced on construction paper
- back cover—any color, 9" x 12" (23 x 30.5 cm) construction paper
- report forms on pages 81 and 82, reproduced for each student
- pencils
- crayons

Steps to Follow

1. Each student or small group of students chooses a type of vehicle to report on from the list on their word bank trains.

2. Read and learn about the vehicle.

3. Complete the report forms. (Even though students may work in a group, each individual will complete the report forms.)

4. Color and cut out the book cover.

5. Use the front cover as a template to trace and cut a back cover from the colored construction paper.

6. Assemble the report between the covers and staple at the top.

The Wheels Go 'Round

My Vehicle Report on

_____

by _____

Draw the vehicle.

Tell what this vehicle looks like.

_____

_____

_____

_____

_____

1

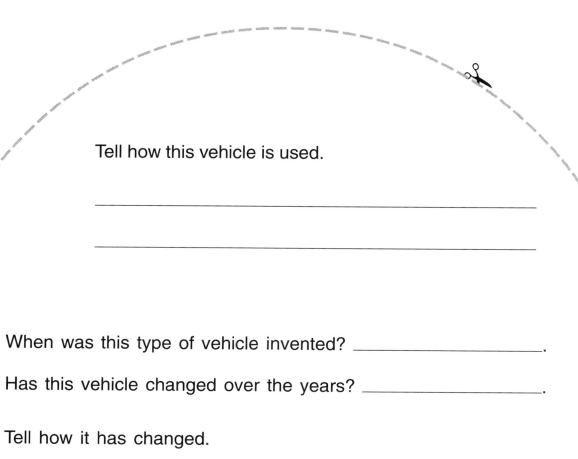

Tell how this vehicle is used.

_____

_____

When was this type of vehicle invented? _____.

Has this vehicle changed over the years? _____.

Tell how it has changed.

_____

_____

_____

2

Sailboat Shape Poems

Build students' vocabulary by reading about sailboats, sharing models of sailboats, and, if possible, watching a video that shows sailboats on the water.

Brainstorm and list many words and phrases that apply to sailboats. Students will choose from this word bank to create their shape poems, so there should be lots of choices. You may have to prompt responses by asking questions—"How does a sailboat move? What do the sails look like? Where is the sailboat?"

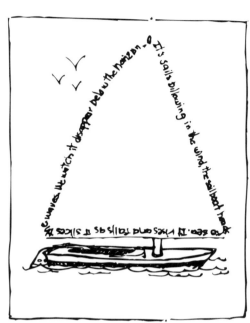

- racing
- gliding
- floating
- bobbing
- rocking
- rising and falling
- slicing the waves
- sails billowing
- chasing the wind
- sleek, colorful sails
- going far away
- crossing the lake
- winning the race

Materials

- boat pattern on page 84, reproduced for each student
- sail pattern on page 85, reproduced for each student
- fine-point black markers
- scissors
- glue
- crayons
- paper clips, 2 per student

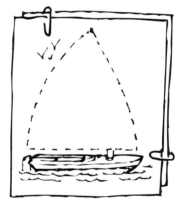

Steps to Follow

1. Put the sail pattern behind the boat pattern and attach it with paper clips.

2. Use the fine-point black marker. With the dark line of the pattern as a guide, write words and phrases from the word bank in the shape of the sail.

3. Color the boat and the background around the sail.

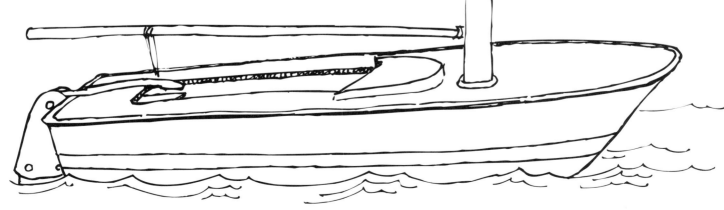

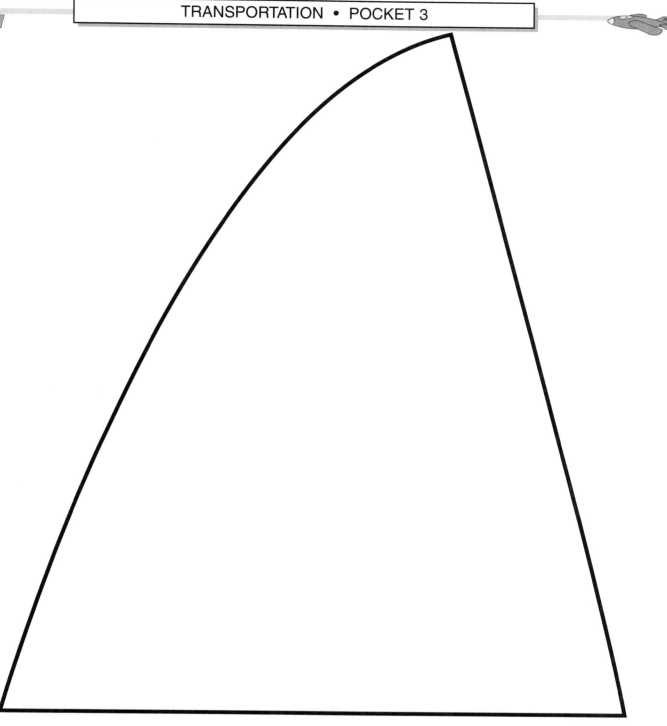

Making Books with Pockets • July • EMC 590

Submarine Shape Book

by Pablo

Before the Lesson

1. Reproduce the word gathering form on page 87 for each student.

2. Ask students what a submarine is. Guide them to understand that the word part (prefix) *sub* means *under*. Explain to the students that they are going to find words that tell that something is *under*.

3. Send the form home with instructions to gather as many words as possible.

4. When forms are returned, compile a composite list on a chart. Note: A number of *sub* words mean *subordinate*, *secondary*, or *less than*. If students mention these, explain that *sub* in these instances has a different meaning so these words will not be added to the chart. Be sure to praise the "word sleuthing" effort, however.

- submarine
- submersible
- submerge
- subterranean
- subsurface
- subway

- underwater
- underground
- underneath
- underside
- undergrowth

- undertow
- underarm
- underfoot
- undergarment
- undersea

Materials

- word gathering form on page 87, reproduced for each student
- front and back covers—submarine pattern on page 88, reproduced on construction paper for each student
- inside pages—submarine pattern on page 88, reproduced on copy paper, 4 per student

- scissors
- pencil
- stapler
- crayons or marking pens

Steps to Follow

1. Cut out the submarine covers and inside pages.

2. Assemble the pages and staple the book together along the top.

3. Title the first two pages—"Words with *Sub*," "Words with *Under*." Write words from the class list on the appropriate page.

4. On the third page write a sentence that contains at least two of the *under* words. For example:

    The submarine submerged and traveled underwater beneath the polar ice.

5. On the final page of the book, draw a picture to illustrate the sentence.

Name: _____

Be a Word Gatherer

How many words can you find that begin with **sub** or **under** and that mean *below* or *beneath*? Ask your family, your friends, and your neighbors.

Words That Begin with *Sub*	Words That Begin with *Under*

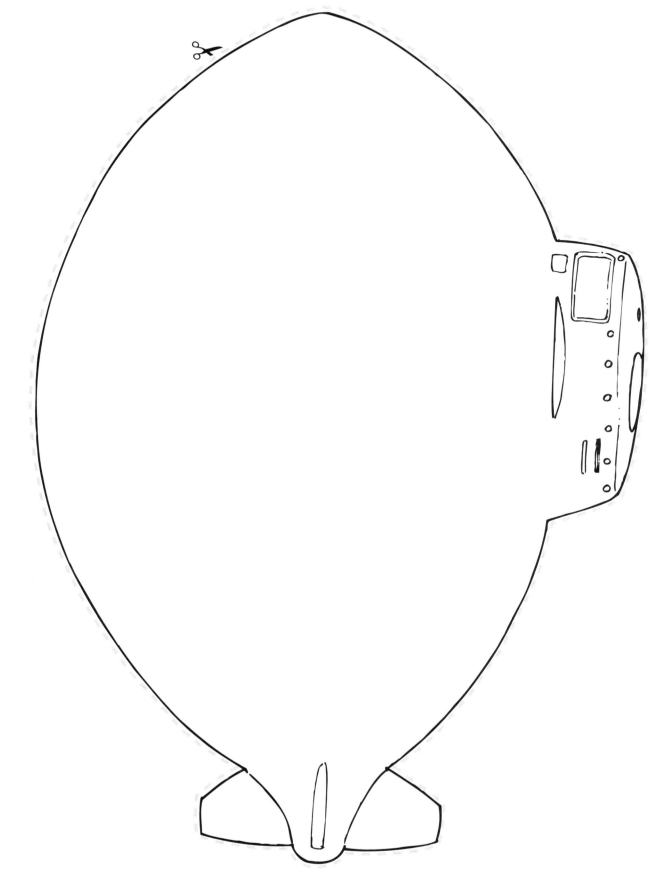

88

Note: Reproduce this page to label each of the three pockets of the *Transportation* Book.

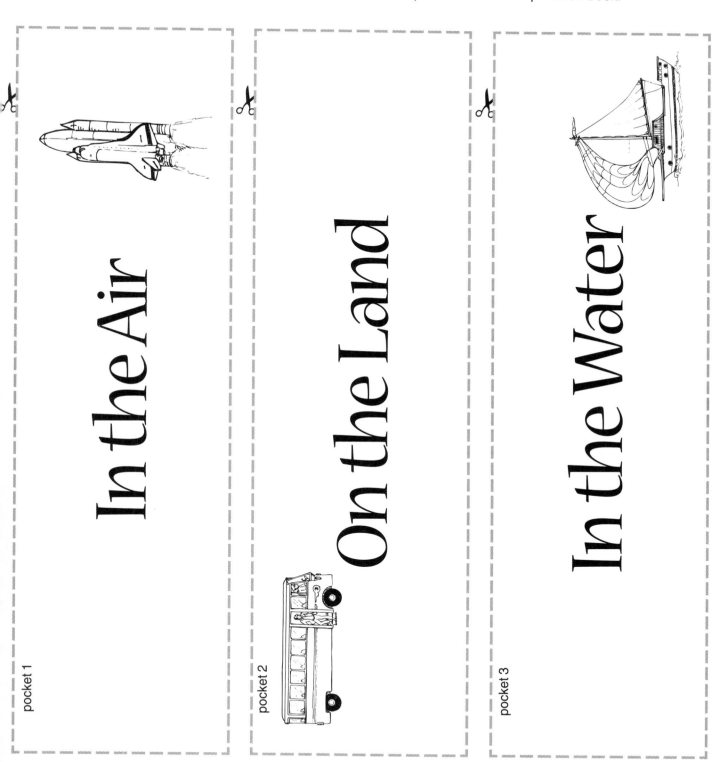

In the Air

pocket 1

On the Land

pocket 2

In the Water

pocket 3

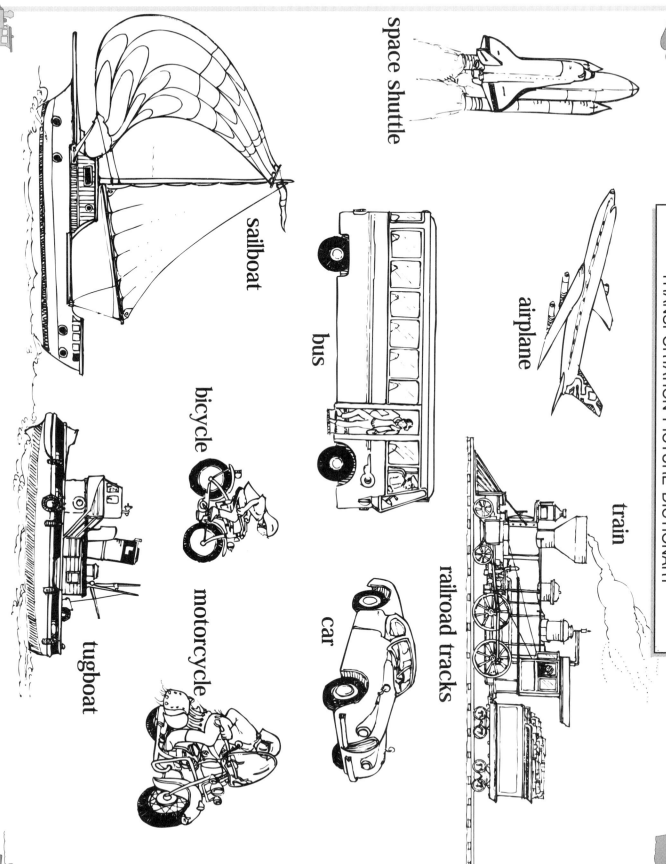

TRANSPORTATION PICTURE DICTIONARY

space shuttle

airplane

sailboat

bus

train

bicycle

railroad tracks

tugboat

motorcycle

car

TRANSPORTATION WRITING FORM

Name: _____

Bulletin Board Bonanza

Shoot for the Stars—pages 93 and 94

Students move their own personal rocket as they work toward reading goals.

Decide how many books you want students to read to "reach the stars." Place signs along the bottom of the bulletin board to indicate each book read. Let's say, for example, if you want students to read 10 books, you might set markers that read: moon; Venus; Mars; asteroid belt; Jupiter's moon, Ganymede; Jupiter; Saturn; Uranus; Neptune. At 10 books, students would reach the stars.

How Have You Traveled?—pages 95 and 96

Students create a class pictograph to show the types of transportation they have used. After the pictograph is created, use it to make comparisons (Have more people traveled by train or by boat?) and for problem solving (How many more people have traveled by car than by airplane?).

Extend the graph work by creating special pictures of each mode of transportation that will stand for five individual pictures. Tell students that you have a way to make it easier to count the pictures on the graph. Model how to replace five pictures with one picture, then let students determine how to do this for the other five means of transportation.

As you work on the pockets of the Space book, use this reading incentive bulletin board to motivate recreational reading.

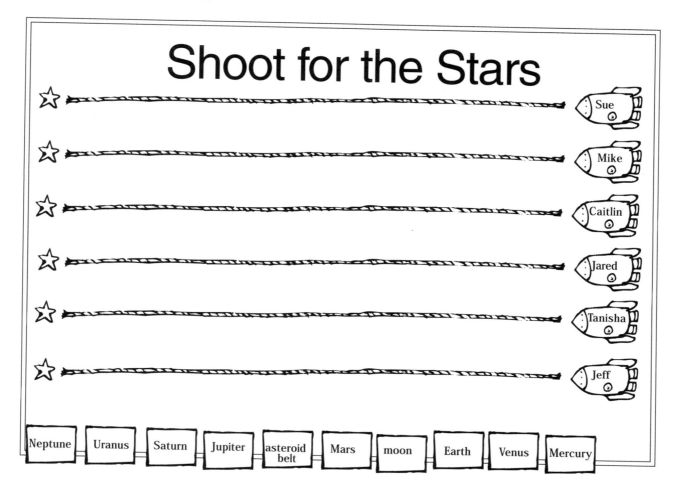

Materials

- butcher paper to back bulletin board
- rocket pattern on page 94, reproduced for each student
- star template on page 94, reproduced for each student
- 4" x 5" (10 x 13 cm) yellow construction paper, one per student
- yarn cut to the length of the bulletin board, one piece per student
- photograph of each student (optional)

Steps to Follow

1. Have students color and cut out their rockets. They are to write their names on them and glue on a photograph if desired.

2. Each student will use the star template to cut out a yellow star.

Making Books with Pockets • July • EMC 590

Star Pattern

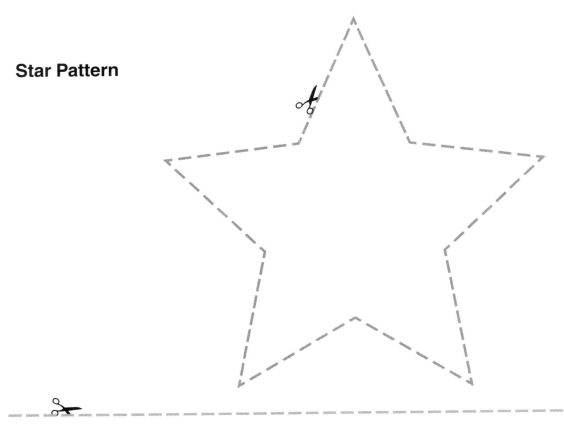

Rocket Pattern

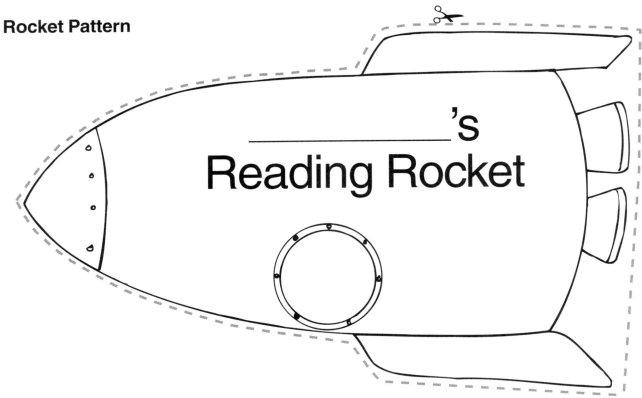

_____'s
Reading Rocket

How Have You Traveled?

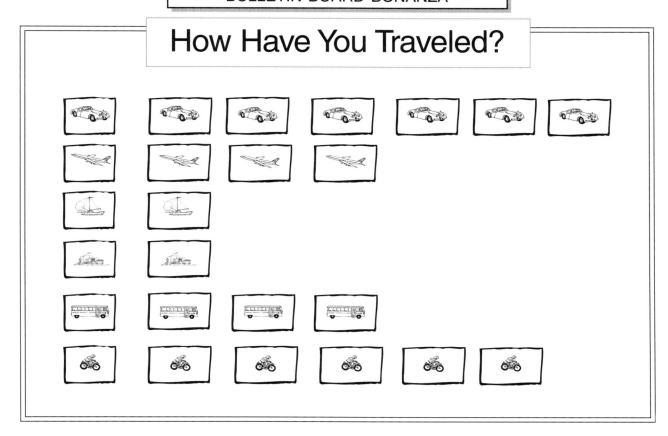

Materials

- light-colored butcher paper
- wide-tipped, black marking pens
- picture cards on page 96, reproduced for each student
- scissors
- push pins

Steps to Follow

1. Set up the bulletin board as shown. Use a set of the picture cards or pictures from your file to label the rows.

2. Direct students to color the picture cards, write their names on the lines, and cut the cards apart.

3. While students are working on other activities, call several students at a time to pin up the picture cards to show the ways in which they have traveled.

_____
name

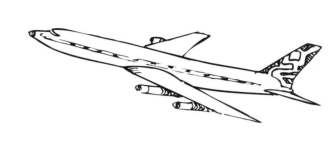

_____
name

_____
name

_____
name

_____
name

_____
name